R.M.S. 'TITAN

A Portrait in Old Picture Postca

by

Mark Bown and Roger Simmons

Foreword by Donald Smith

Brampton Publications
1987

First published in 1987 by Brampton Publications.

℅ 5 Queen Margaret's Road, Loggerheads, Nr. Market Drayton, Shropshire, TF9 4EP.

British Library Cataloguing in Publication Data

Bown, Mark
R.M.S. 'TITANIC' : a portrait in old picture postcards.
1. Titanic *(Ship)* – Pictorial works
2. Postal cards
I. Title II. Simmons, Roger
769'.437 VK1255.T6

ISBN 0 9511469 5 5

Represented in Great Britain by Sidgwick and Jackson Ltd.,
1 Tavistock Chambers, Bloomsbury Way, London WC1A 2SG.

Distributed by Macmillan Distribution Ltd.,
Houndmills Estate, Basingstoke, Hampshire RG21 2XS.

Printed in Great Britain by Rubell Print Ltd., Bunbury, Tarporley, Cheshire, CW6 9PQ.

Bound by J W Braithwaite and Son Limited, Pountney Street, Wolverhampton WV2 4HY.

CONTENTS

CONTENTS CONTINUED

FOREWORD

by

Donald Smith, great nephew to Captain E. J. Smith, Master of the 'Titanic'

I am delighted to have been asked to write a foreword to this new book about the 'Titanic', illustrating the story of this great ship on old picture postcards.

My earliest recollection of the existence and fame of my great uncle, Captain Edward John Smith, was a visit to Lichfield in Staffordshire to view the statue in Beacon Park, when I was seven years old. I often return to visit the statue and always gain a great sense of pride seeing the Captain there. I was very interested to discover that the statue was sculptured by Lady Kathleen Scott, wife to Captain Robert Scott, the famous British Antartic explorer.

In 1985, I started a campaign to have the statue returned to Hanley, Stoke-on-Trent, the home town of Capt. Smith. I wrote to Stoke City Council with this idea in mind and in September of the same year, they approched Lichfield District Council and formally asked for the statue to be returned. I had offered to pay for the cost of transportation. Unfortunately, this request was refused by Lichfield Council in 1986. This was naturally a great disappointment because my family would dearly love to see the statue brought back to the Potteries, where it rightfully belongs.

I am very fortunate to own some of my great uncle's possessions, which include one of his sextants, the telescope that he used when he was Master of the 'Olympic', a pocket watch and one of his cigar holders in its original case.

I wish Brampton Publications every success with this new book and may the memory of the 'Titanic' live on forever.

Donald Smith,
Hanley, Stoke-on-Trent.

INTRODUCTION

The loss of the 'Titanic' on Monday, 15th April, 1912 has remained the world's worst maritime disaster during peacetime. Public interest and debate concerning the loss of the luxury White Star passenger liner, at the time the world's largest ship, has continued over the last seventy five years and in particular, following the rediscovery of her last resting place by the Woods Hole Oceanographic Team in 1985 and again in 1986.

Many excellent and authoritative books have been written about the 'Titanic' and the aim of this book is to illustrate the story of the ship, but using old picture postcards, which have become some of the rarest and most valuable postcards collected today.

The authors have selected the best postcards from their collections and follow in sequence the building, launch, trials, maiden voyage and disaster of the 'Titanic'. These are followed by a selection of 'In Memoriam' postcards and some unusual postcards published after the loss of the ship.

During the Edwardian era, known to postcard collectors as the 'Golden Age of Postcards', a national craze of collecting postcards existed in this country. Postcard publishers produced vast numbers of cards depicting every subject imaginable, and naturally a national disaster was a prime subject to feature. The national craze died out with the commencement of the First World War and postcard sales dropped dramatically with the rise in postage rates and the increased use of the telephone. Many collections were forgotten but were rediscovered when the hobby started to become popular in the mid 1970's. During the last ten years it has become one of the fastest growing collecting hobbies, with new collectors joining the hobby annually.

Amongst the more sought after postcards are those depicting the 'Titanic'. The rarest cards are those that were issued and postally used before the date of the disaster. After 15th April, 1912, postcard publishers issued a wide variety of postcards. These more common and less valuable cards can offer a fascinating study to the story of the 'Titanic', with publishers even printing incorrect details about the ship.

The postcards illustrated in this book are not a definitive list, but offer collectors an idea to the range of postcards available. The authors would be pleased to learn of any new postcards owned by other collectors not featured in this book.

Mark Bown and Roger Simmons
July 1987.

WHITE STAR OFFICES, LIVERPOOL

The offices of the White Star Line in Britain were based in Liverpool.
The company was owned by and part of the giant International Mercantile Marine Company, founded by J. P. Morgan and whose president was Joseph Bruce Ismay. Fierce competition existed for the lucrative trans-Atlantic passenger market and following Cunard's success with the 'Lusitania' and 'Mauretania' both launched in 1906, White Star planned in early 1907 to build two giant luxury liners (later joined by a third), providing a weekly express service from Southampton to New York. These ships were named 'Olympic', 'Titanic' and 'Gigantic' (the latter subsequently changed to Britannic).

(Published by Valentines – M. Bown collection)

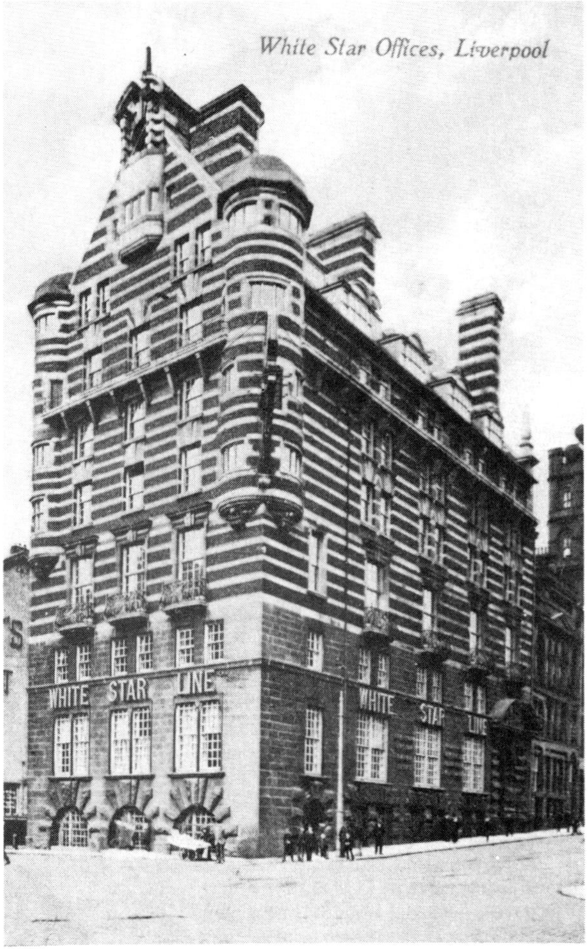

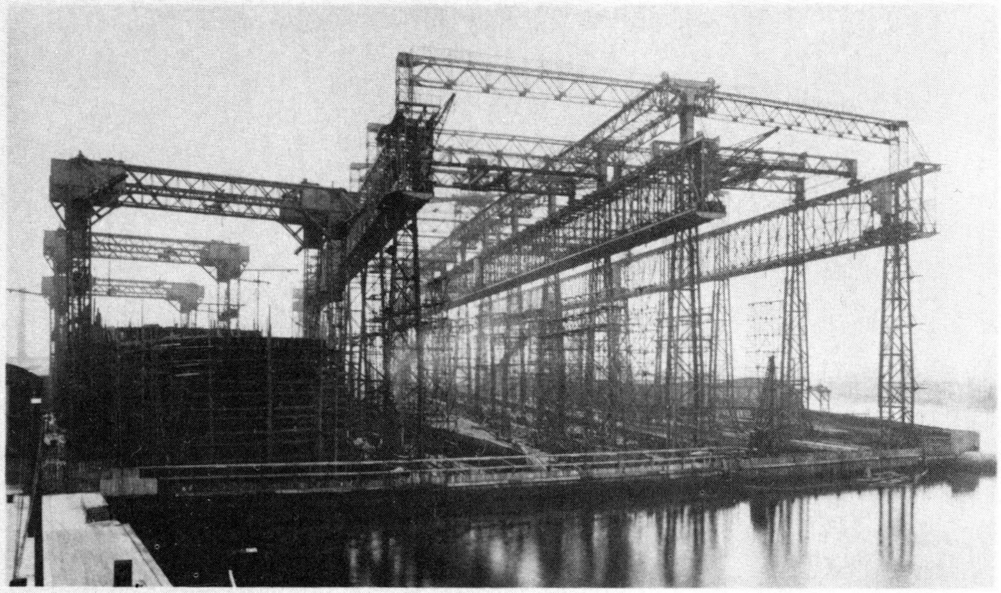

No. 66 HARLAND & WOLFF'S SHIPBUILDING YARD FROM VICTORIA WHARF, BELFAST.

HARLAND AND WOLFF'S SHIPYARD, QUEEN'S ISLAND, BELFAST

Harland and Wolff, the Belfast Shipbuilders were chosen to build the three new ships, through their close association with White Star and having built the majority of the company's ships. The Chairman of Harland and Wolff, Lord Pirrie would be responsible for their design and the Rt. Hon. Alexander Carlisle would be responsible for the general construction, decoration and equipment. The order was placed for the 'Olympic' and 'Titanic' on 1st July, 1907 and the two ships were given the shipyard numbers 400 and 401 respectively.

Major alterations were made at the shipyard with two special slipways constructed, numbers 2 and 3. These were in turn surmounted by an enormous Arrol gantry, built especially for the construction of the two ships. The 'Olympic's' keel was laid on 1st January, 1909 and its outline can be seen in the centre of the postcard. To the right, preparations are being made for the 'Titanic's' keel, which was laid on 31st March, 1909.

(Published by Hurst & Co., Belfast – M. Bown collection)

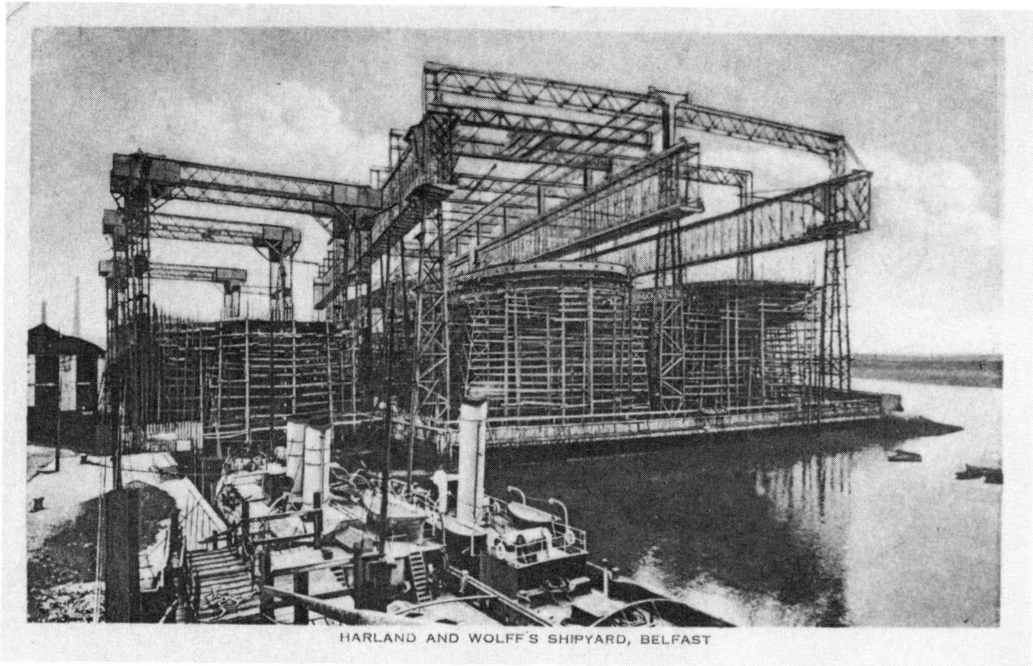

HARLAND & WOLFF'S SHIPYARD, BELFAST

The two ships were constructed side by side, with the 'Olympic's' progress a few months ahead of the 'Titanic'. Following the two keels being laid, the vertical keels and then the floors were positioned. This was followed by the framing, which was completed on the 'Olympic' by 20th November, 1909. Interior work on the beams, deck plating and shell plating was completed on the 'Olympic' by April, 1910. By this date, the 'Titanic' had been fully framed. The postcard illustrates the stern view of both ships, at this stage of the construction.

(Published by W. R. and S. 'Reliable' series – M. Bown collection)

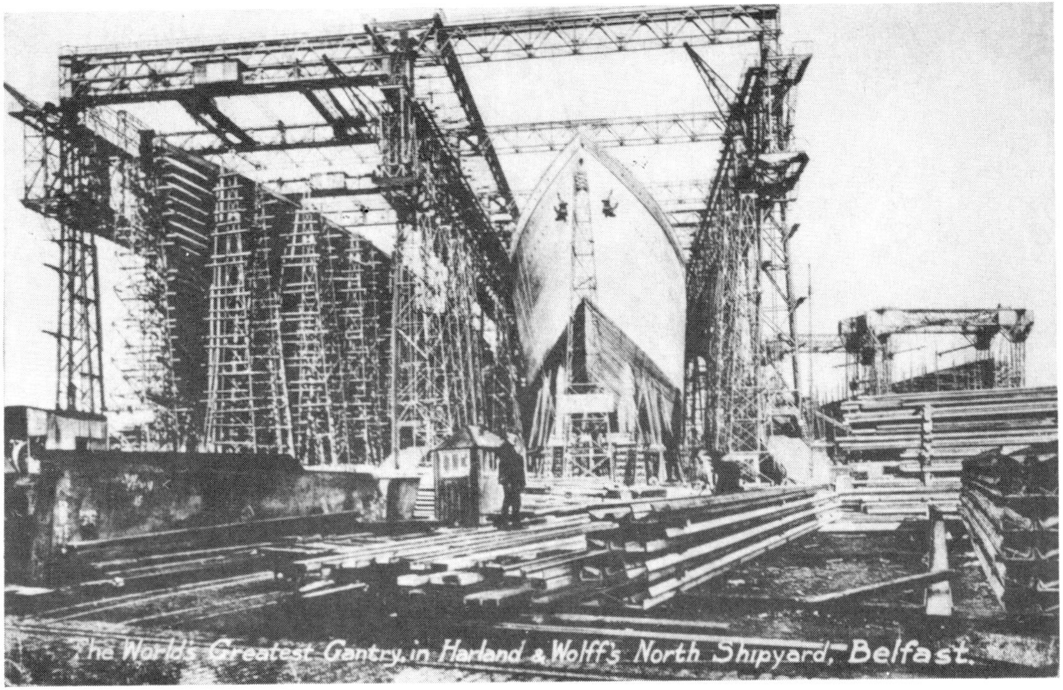

HARLAND AND WOLFF'S SHIPYARD, BELFAST

A forward view of the two giant sister ships with the framed 'Titanic' on the left, and the 'Olympic' nearing completion on the right.

The Arrol gantry built for the construction of the two ships consisted of three rows of towers spaced 121 ft. between the rows, and each row having eleven towers, spaced 80 ft. apart.

The top of the towers were connected by girders fore and aft and mounted on the structure were one central revolving crane, ten walking cranes and six travelling frames, three over each berth and each carrying two cranes. Access to the structure was by four lifts and inclined walkways. The total area exceeded 840 ft. long by 270 ft. wide. The total height was 228 ft. and the weight of the entire structure was 6000 tons.

(Published by Philco – M. Bown collection)

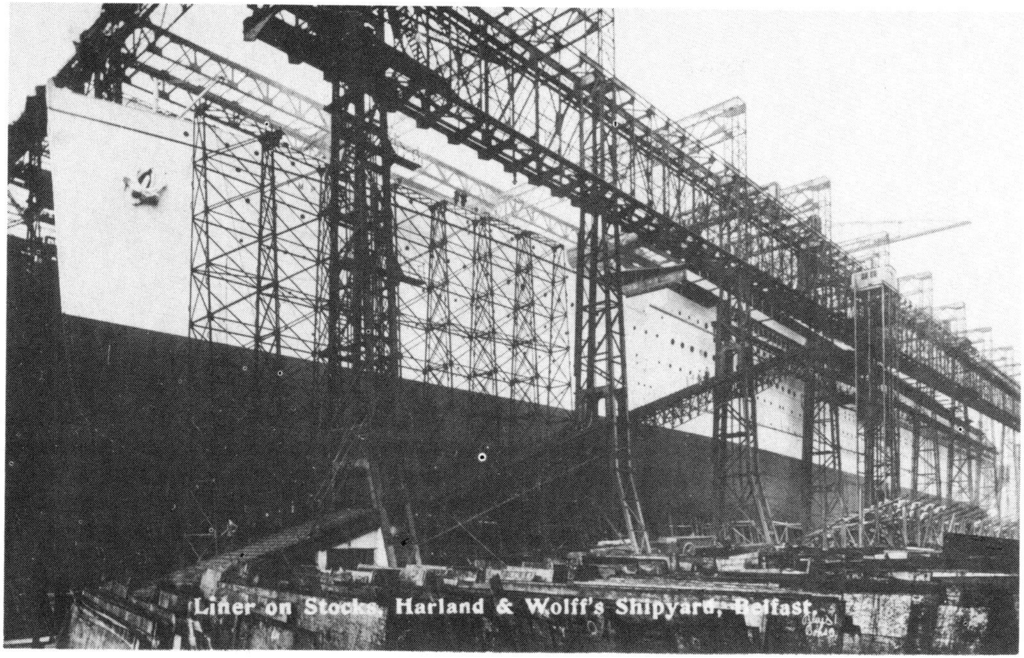

HARLAND AND WOLFF SHIPYARD, BELFAST

The 'Olympic' on the stocks prior to her launch, with shipyard workers visible on the deck and walkways, dwarfed by the huge size of the hull.

After ten months from the keel being laid, the 'Olympic' was launched on 20th October, 1910 in the presence of the Lord Lieutenant of Ireland, J. Pierpoint Morgan and J. Bruce Ismay. The launch took just 62 seconds to complete. After the launch, the 'Olympic' was moored at the deep water wharf for the fitting of its machinery and then taken to the graving dock on 1st April, 1911, for its final fitting out.

It was completed by the end of May, 1911, just over seven months from the launch.

(Published by W. E. Walton, Belfast – M. Bown collection)

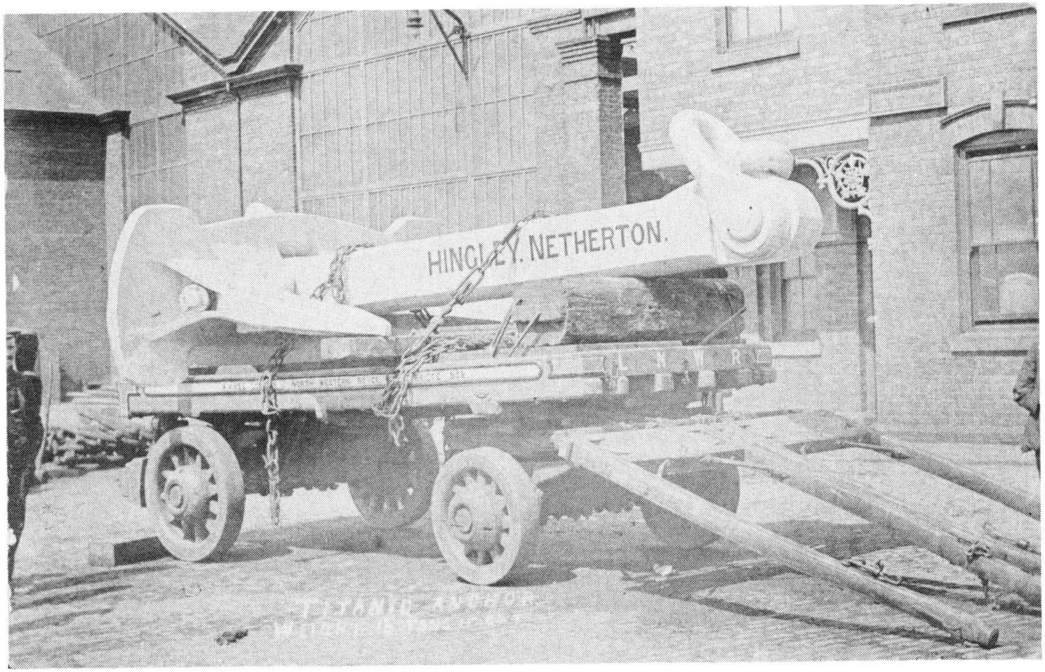

THE 'TITANIC' CENTRE ANCHOR

The centre anchor was made to Hall's stockless patent design by Messrs. N. Hingley and Sons Ltd., of Netherton, Dudley, and weighed 16 tons 11 cwt. Due to the size of the 'Titanic', the centre anchor was made to supplement the two side bower anchors, each weighing 7¾ tons, and was positioned in a well immediately below the stem. A crane was fitted on the forecastle for lifting the anchor and the wire hawser, which led through an extra hawsepipe in the stem, was made to 9½″ circumference, 175 fathoms long and supplied by Messrs. Bullivant of London.

The photograph shows the anchor loaded on its carriage prior to despatch for Belfast from Hingley's works.

(Publisher unknown – M. Bown collection)

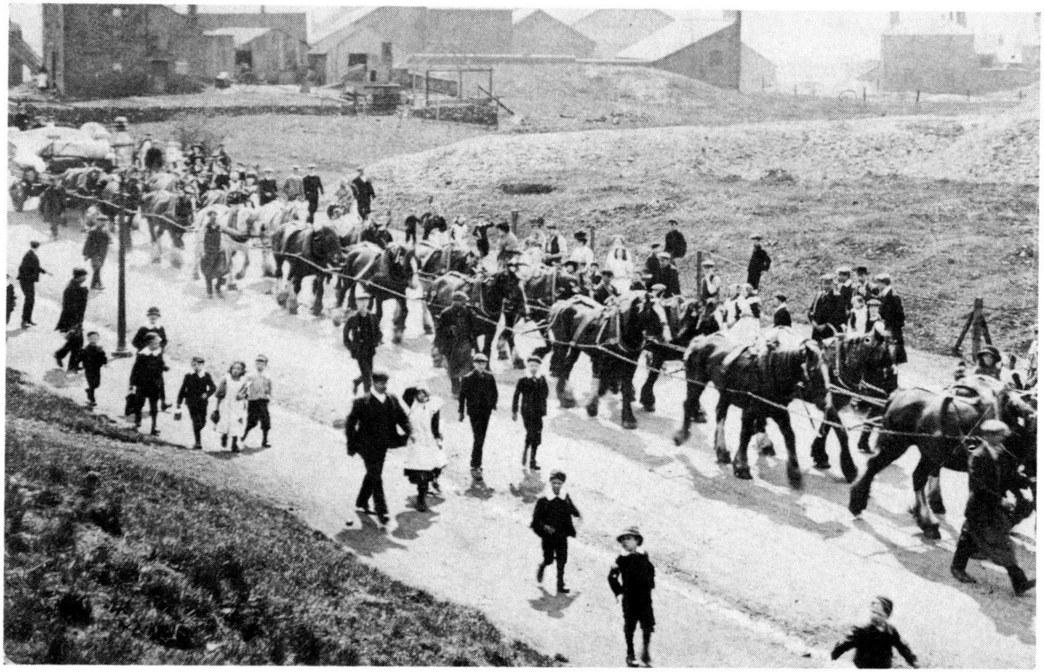

THE 'TITANIC' CENTRE ANCHOR

When the centre anchor was despatched from Hingley's works, a twenty-horse team was required to transport it to the nearest rail sidings for carriage to Harland and Wolff's yard in Belfast. All three anchors were fitted before the launch.

(Published by E. Beech, Cradley Heath – M. Bown collection)

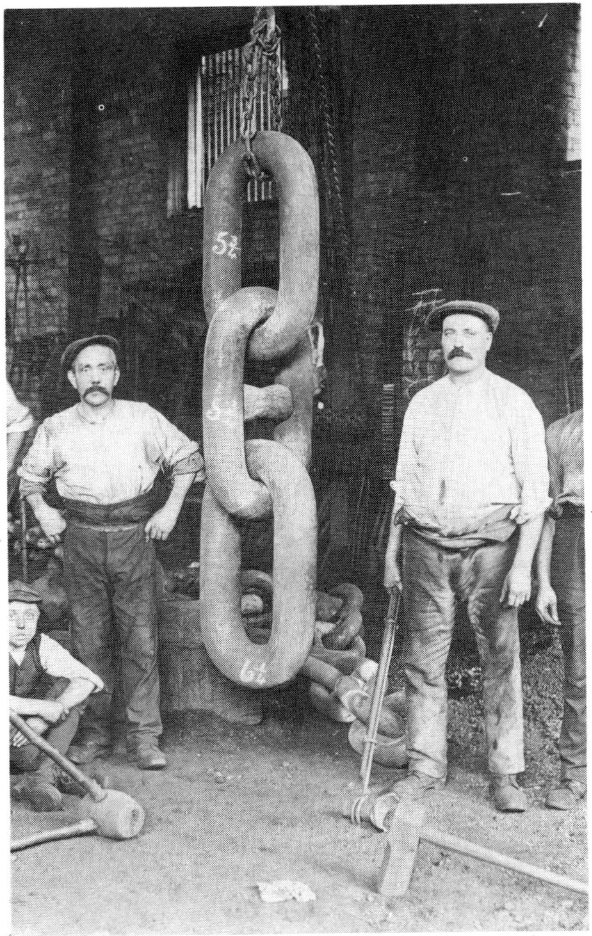

THE 'TITANIC' CENTRE ANCHOR'S CABLE

The cable links for the centre anchor were also made by N. Hingley & Sons Ltd. This interesting postcard shows the comparison in size of the links to some of the men, who forged them.
The links were 5¾″ and 6¼″ diameter and at the time were the largest links ever made.

(Published by E. Beech, Cradley Heath – M. Bown collection)

THE 'TITANIC' CENTRE ANCHOR'S CABLE

A further comparison of the cable size with its necessary swivel arrangement, to one of the foundry workers at Hingley's works.

(Published by E. Beech, Cradley Heath – M. Bown collection)

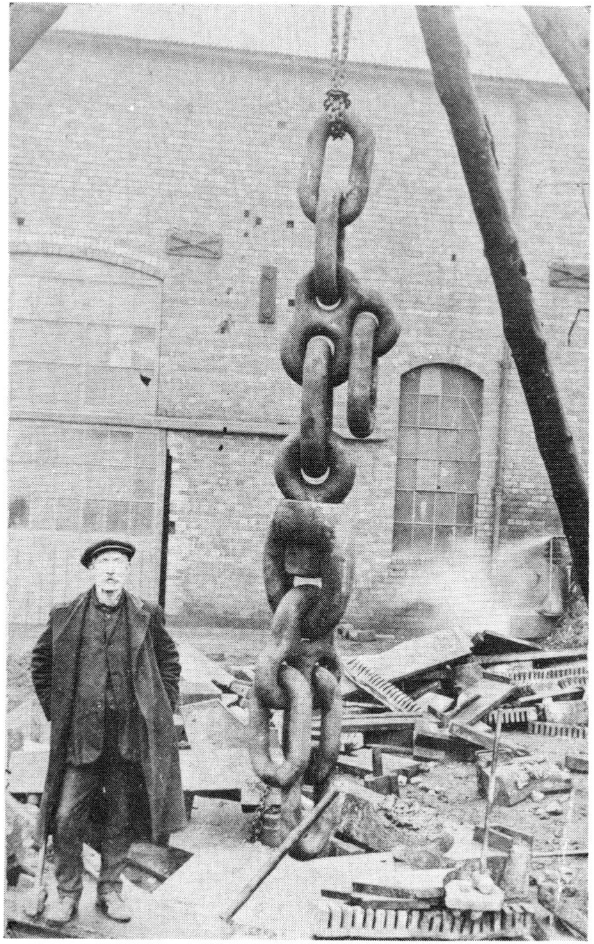

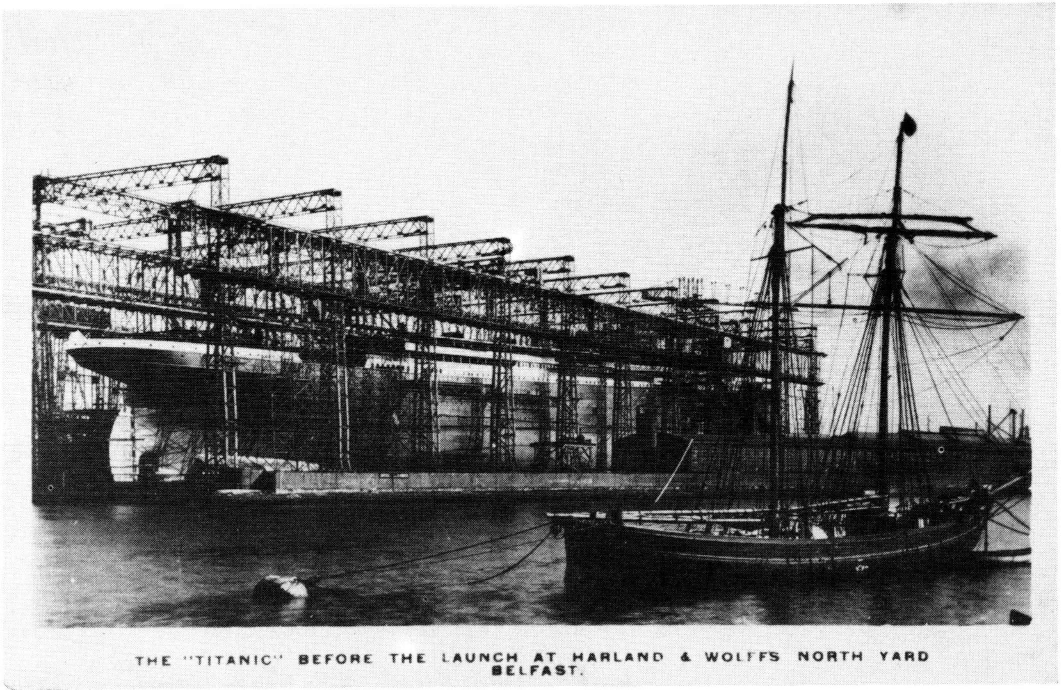

HARLAND AND WOLFF'S SHIPYARD, BELFAST

The 'Titanic' nearing completion under the deserted gantry in the empty shipyard, suggesting that this photograph was taken on a Sunday, shortly before the launch.

During the construction of the 'Titanic', the shipyard ensured the highest standards of design and used hydraulic riveting to give the best quality plating, which was completed by 19th October, 1910.

The total cost of the 'Titanic', including equipment was approximately £1,500,000.

(Published by Hurst & Co., Belfast – R. Simmons collection)

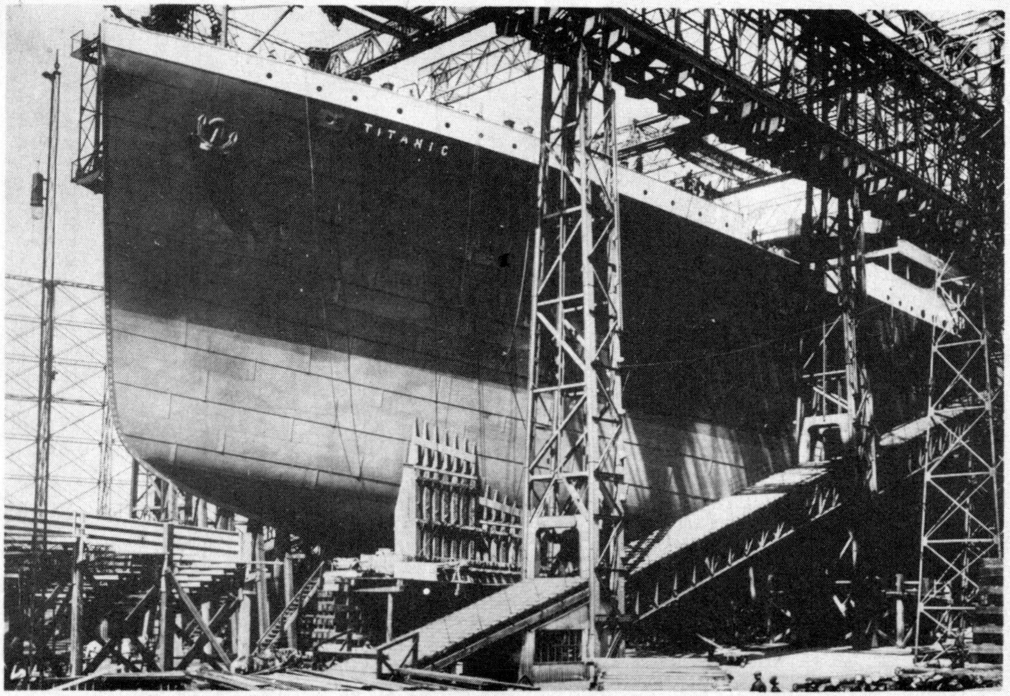

THE IMMENSE GANTRY AT HARLAND & WOLFF'S SHIPBUILDING WORKS, BELFAST, WITH THE WORLD'S BIGGEST SHIP "TITANIC" JUST READY TO LAUNCH.

THE LAUNCH OF THE 'TITANIC'

Final preparations are made before the launch of the 'Titanic'.
The photograph clearly shows the plating arrangement to the hull, and the forward launching cradle and bracket assembly by the gantry's inclined walkway. The two hydraulic launching triggers that held the vessel when all the shores and blocks were removed, were positioned close to the launching cradle.
In the left foreground can be seen the temporary platform for the dignitaries to view the launch.

(Published as a Book Postcard (7¼″ × 5¼″) by James Doherty, Belfast – M. Bown collection)

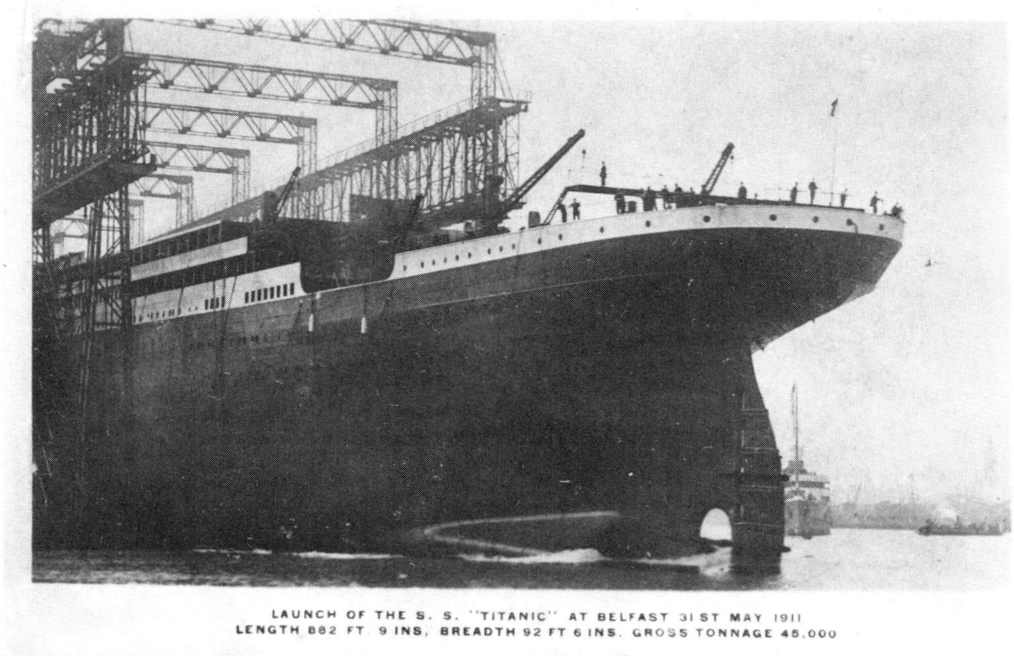

THE LAUNCH OF THE 'TITANIC'

The 'Titanic' was launched on 31st May, 1911 at 12.15 p.m. The whole procedure took 62 seconds and was witnessed by more than 100,000 people, including J. Pierpont Morgan and J. Bruce Ismay.

The quantity of lubricants used during the launch included twenty three tons of tallow, train oil and soft soap. Controlling her speed down the slip were 3 anchors each side and 80 tons of cable.

(Published by Hurst & Co., Belfast – M. Bown collection)

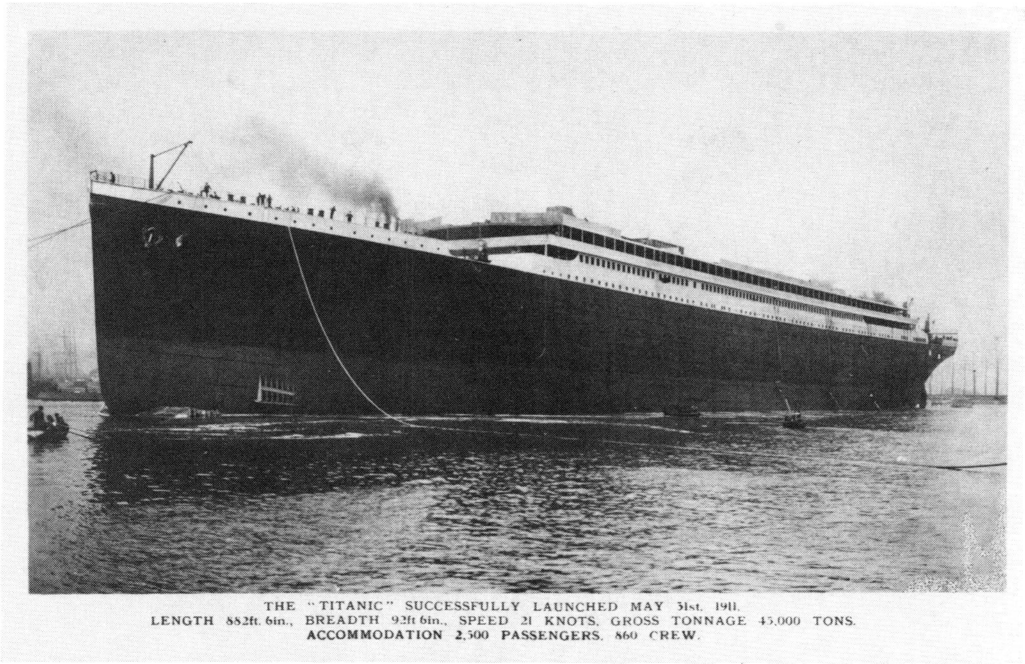

THE LAUNCH OF THE 'TITANIC'

The 'Titanic' afloat on the river Lagan after the successful launch and waiting to be towed away from the slipway. The launch date also coincided with the departure of the 'Olympic' to Liverpool, following the successful completion of her trials the previous day.

(Published by Walton, Belfast – R. Simmons collection)

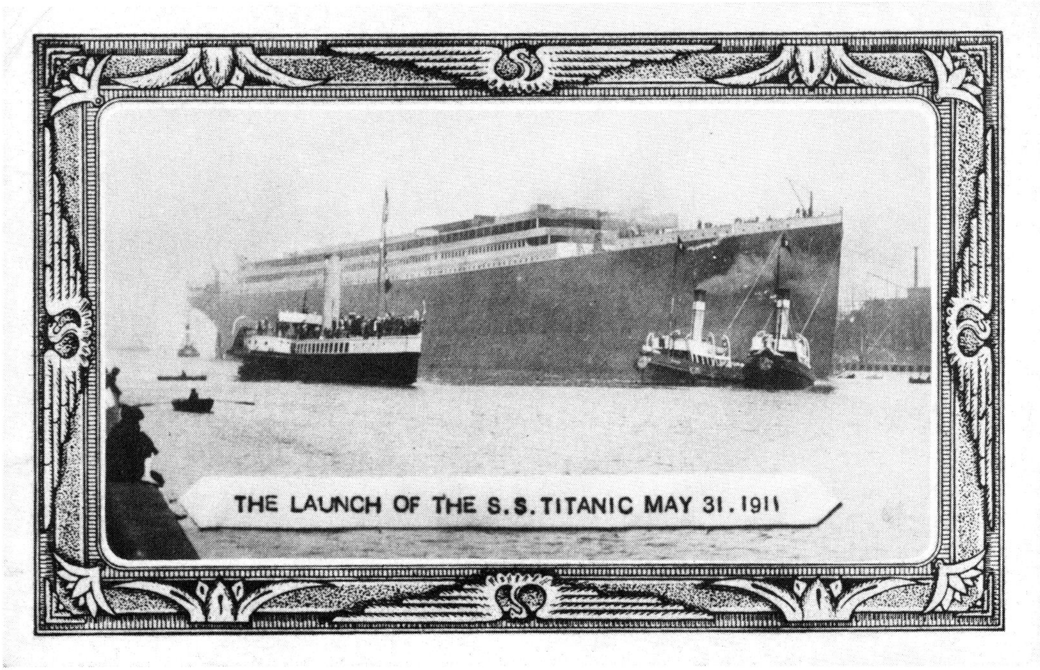

LAUNCH OF THE 'TITANIC'

Five tugs were used to manoeuvre the 'Titanic' after the launch, and this rare photograph shows the 'Titanic' being towed to its deep water berth for the fitting out.

Note also the crowded decks of the paddle steamer listing to port with the fortunate passengers having had a close up view of the launch.

(Published by J. Johnson, Belfast – R. Simmons collection)

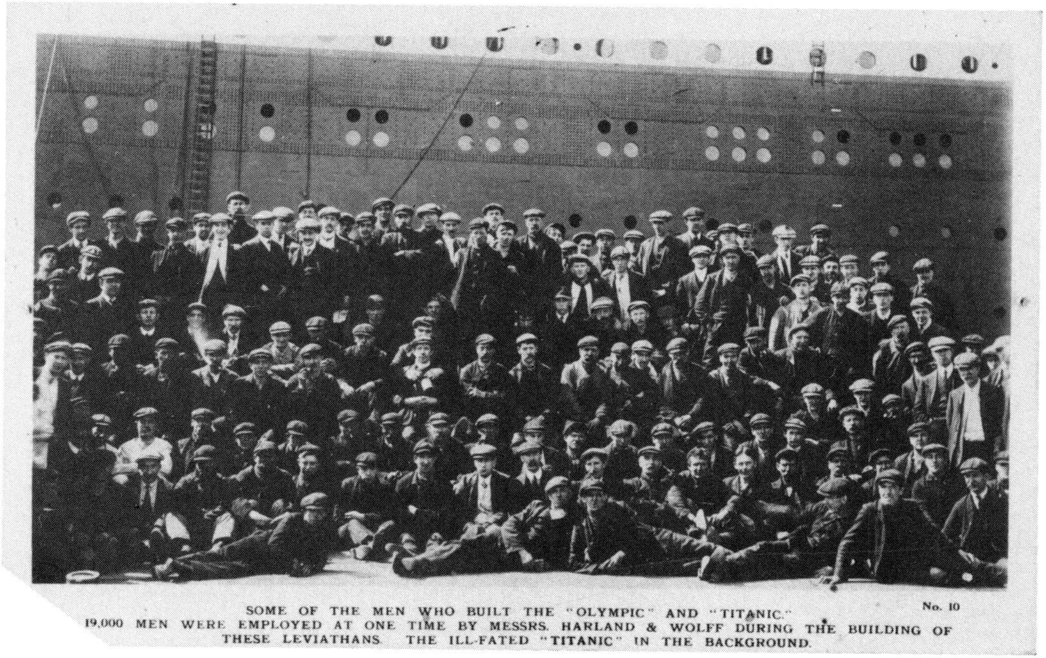

THE FITTING OUT OF THE 'TITANIC'

Some of the 19,000 men employed by Harland & Wolff, who built the 'Olympic' and the 'Titanic', and assembled for this photograph at the fitting out basin, with the 'Titanic' in the background. All the equipment, machinery, interior decorations and final construction to her superstructure would be carried out here.

In comparison to the 'Olympic', slight modifications were made to her design resulting in her becoming the largest passenger vessel in the world.

(Published by Walton, Belfast – M. Bown collection)

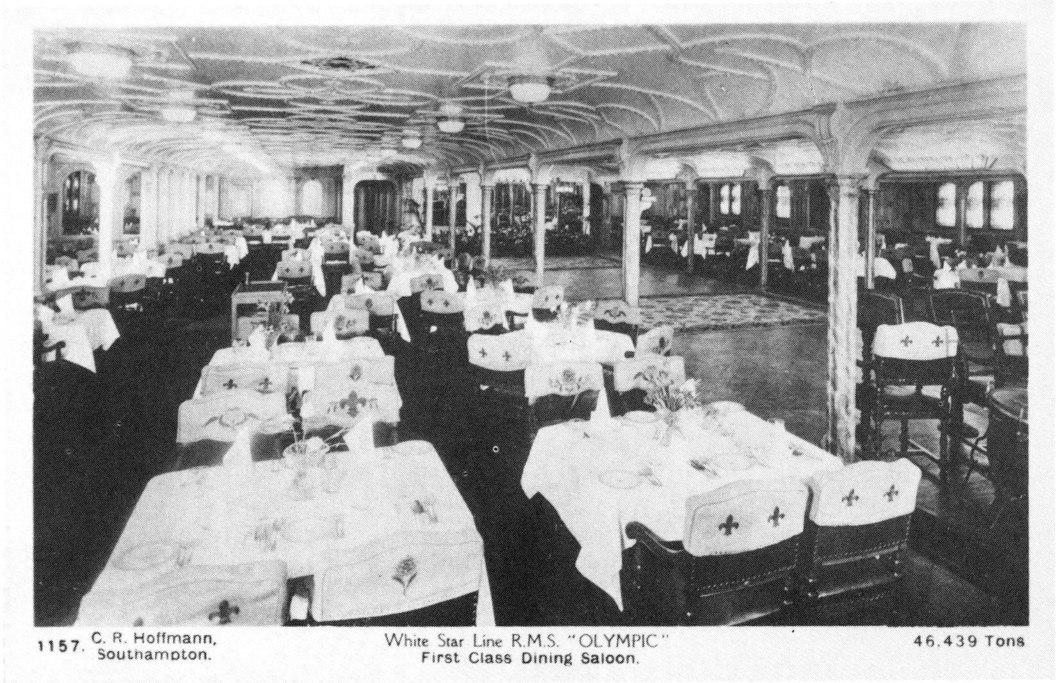

FIRST-CLASS PASSENGER ACCOMMODATION

Both the 'Olympic' and 'Titanic' were fitted out to the same magnificent standard. As postcard interior views of the 'Titanic' are extremely rare, six postcards of the 'Olympic's' interior have been featured to illustrate the luxury that the passengers on the 'Titanic' would have experienced. The first-class accommodation equalling the finest hotels, extended over five decks with access between decks provided by two grand staircases, stairways and three electric lifts. The first-class public rooms included the dining saloon, reception room, restaurant, lounge, reading and writing room, smoking room and a verandah café, known as the Café Parisien. The dining saloon viewed above was 114 ft. long by 92 ft. wide (the full width of the ship). It was decorated in Jacobean style based on observations of Haddon Hall, with the walls and ceilings painted white. Dining accommodation was provided for 532 passengers.

(Published by C. R. Hoffman, Southampton – M. Bown collection)

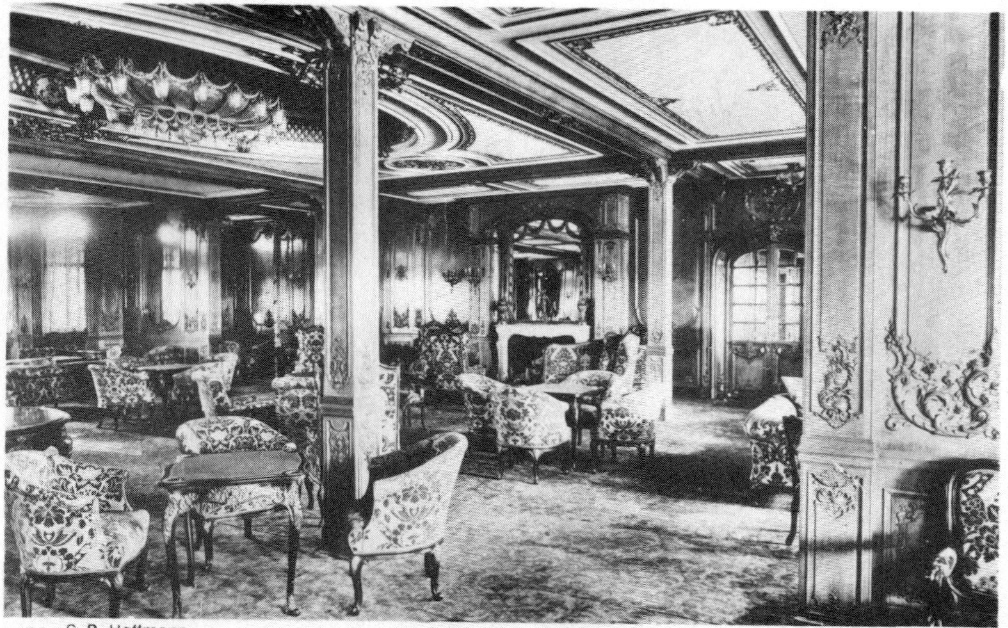

1161. C. R. Hoffmann, Southampton. White Star Line R.M.S. "OLYMPIC" First Class Lounge. 46,439 Tons.

FIRST-CLASS PASSENGER ACCOMMODATION

The first-class lounge was situated on the promenade deck and decorated in the Louis Quinze style, based on observations of the Palace at Versailles.
The lounge was 59 ft. long, 63 ft. wide and 12 ft. 3" high.
To the left of the picture and directly opposite the fireplace was a large bookcase.
Behind the finely carved wall on the right was the reading and writing room.
(Published by C. R. Hoffman, Southampton – M. Bown collection)

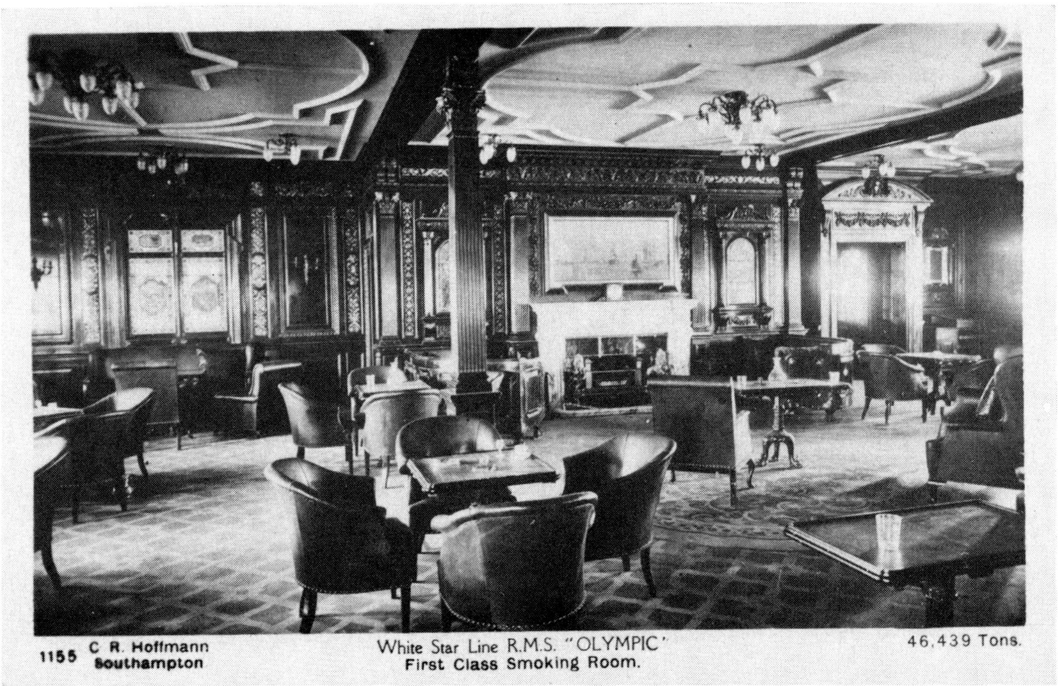

FIRST-CLASS PASSENGER ACCOMMODATION

The first-class smoking room was situated towards the after-end of the promenade deck. It was designed in an early Georgian style and based on observations of houses of that period. The smoking room was 65 ft. long, 63 ft. wide and 12 ft. 3″ high, with the walls panelled with mahogany. The door in the right background led to the verandahs and palm courts. Additional first-class features included a gymnasium, squash court, Turkish bath and a swimming pool.

(Published by C. R. Hoffman, Southampton – M. Bown collection)

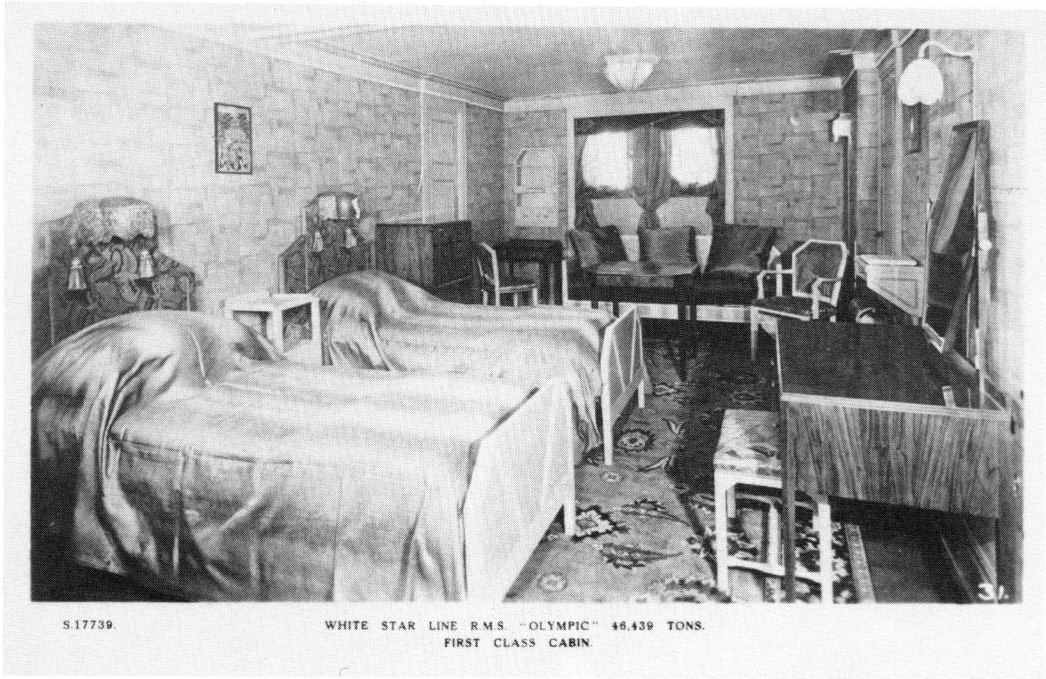

FIRST-CLASS PASSENGER ACCOMMODATION

The first-class cabin accommodation consisted of 96 one berth, 106 two berth and 127 three berth state rooms, plus 4 Parlour Suite sitting rooms, accommodating a total number of 735 first class passengers.
All the state rooms were very luxurious and designed in a variety of period styles.
The postcard illustration of a first-class two berth cabin, was photographed at a later stage in the life of the 'Olympic' but does give an idea to the size of the cabins.

(M. Bown collection)

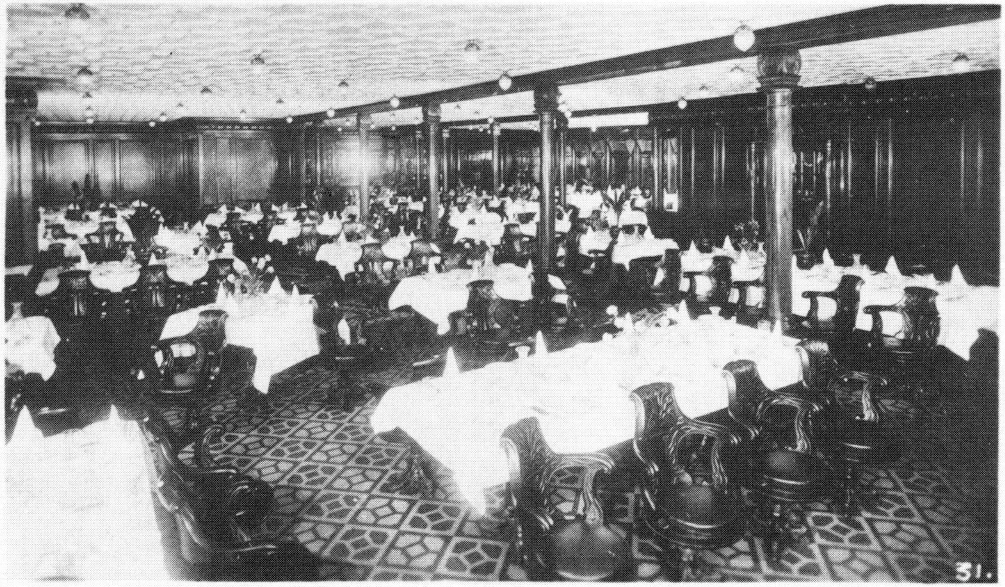

S.17741. WHITE STAR LINE R.M.S. "OLYMPIC" 46,439 TONS.
SECOND CLASS DINING SALOON.

SECOND-CLASS PASSENGER ACCOMMODATION

The second-class accommodation extended over seven decks in the after-end of the ship, with access between the decks by a grand staircase and an electric lift. The public rooms included a large dining saloon, smoking room and library. There were also 207 second-class bedrooms for 674 passengers.
The dining saloon viewed above was on the saloon deck, close to the kitchen.
It was 71 ft. long and extended the full width of the ship.
It was decorated in an Early English style with oak panelling and provided seating for 394 people.

(M. Bown collection)

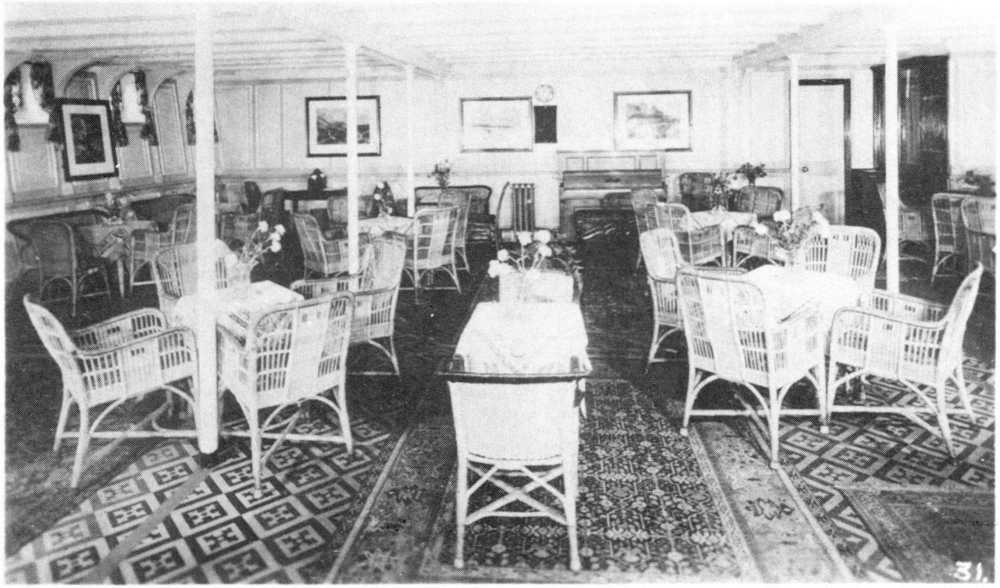

S.17742. WHITE STAR LINE R.M.S. "OLYMPIC" 46,439 TONS.
TOURIST THIRD CABIN LOUNGE.

THIRD-CLASS PASSENGER ACCOMMODATION

The third-class accommodation was of a very high standard. The public rooms included a dining saloon, seating 473 passengers, a general room and a smoking room, which were both situated on opposite sides of the poop deck. There were 222 bedrooms accommodating 862 passengers and open berths for 164 passengers. The third-class lounge viewed above is a later illustration of the original third-class general room. It was 36 ft. long and 38 ft. wide, panelled in pine and finished in white enamel. The original seating consisted of long wooden settees, tables and chairs.

(M. Bown collection)

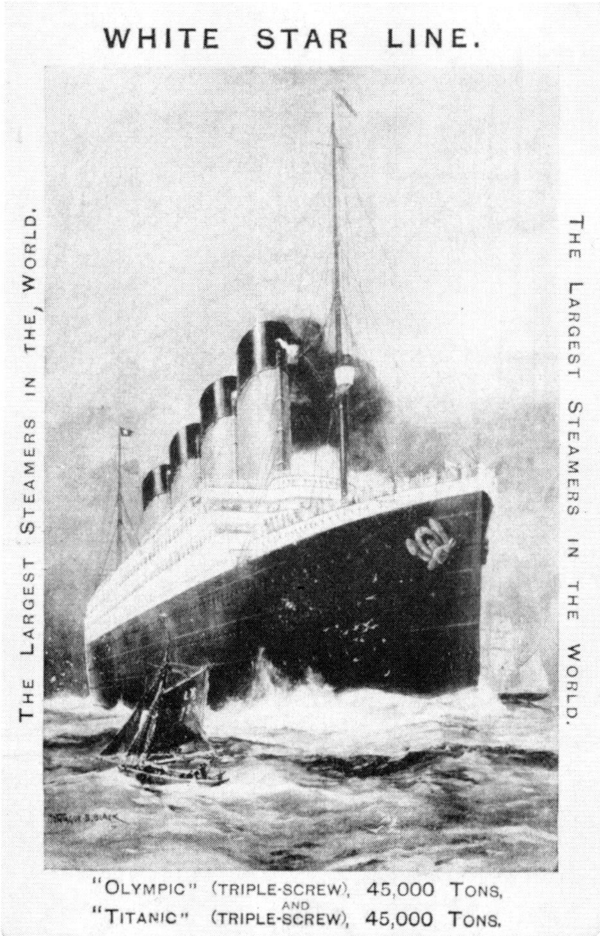

STATISTICS OF THE 'TITANIC'

Length 882 ft. 9 ins;
Breadth 92 ft. 6 ins;
Height from keel to bridge 73 ft. 3 ins;
Draught 34 ft. 6 ins;
Gross tonnage 46,328 tons;
Reciprocating engines providing 46,000 H.P. and driving two outer propellers and one centre 'ahead only' propeller.
The engines were powered by 24 double and five single-ended boilers.
The design incorporated a double bottom, with sixteen watertight compartments, with the ship capable of still floating with any two of these compartments flooded.
The 'unsinkable' ships were built with maximum safety and comfort for the passengers. The ships were designed and capable of moderate speeds to ensure and eliminate unnecessary vibration.
Only 16 wooden lifeboats and 4 collapsible canvas lifeboats were installed, giving a maximum carrying capacity of 1,167 persons. (Her passenger certificate stated that she could carry a total of 3,547 persons, passengers and crew).
During the building of the two ships, White Star's publicity department issued this postcard based on a painting by Montague Black, to advertise the new luxury service to New York.

(M. Bown collection)

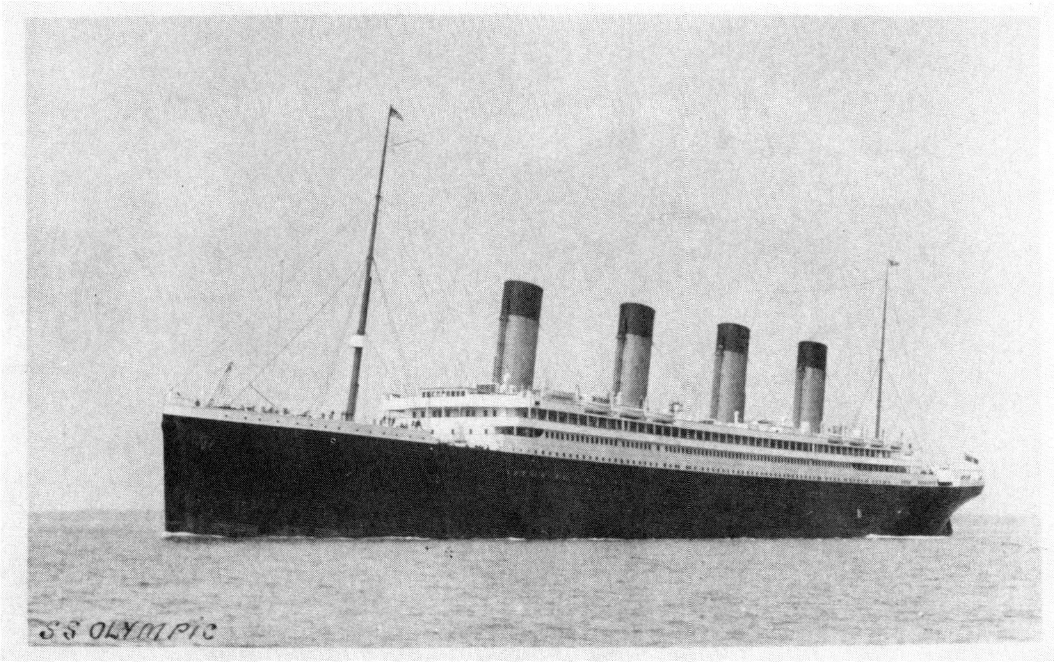

R.M.S. 'OLYMPIC'

After leaving Belfast on 31st May, 1911, the 'Olympic' proceeded to Southampton, via Liverpool, arriving on 2nd June, 1911. She was the first ship to use the new White Star dock, which had been built to accommodate these extra large vessels.

On 14th June, 1912, the 'Olympic' sailed on her maiden voyage to New York averaging 21.17 knots on her outward passage and 22.32 knots on her return.

This is an early photograph of the 'Olympic' as the ship still has a single row of lifeboats.

(Publisher unknown – M. Bown collection)

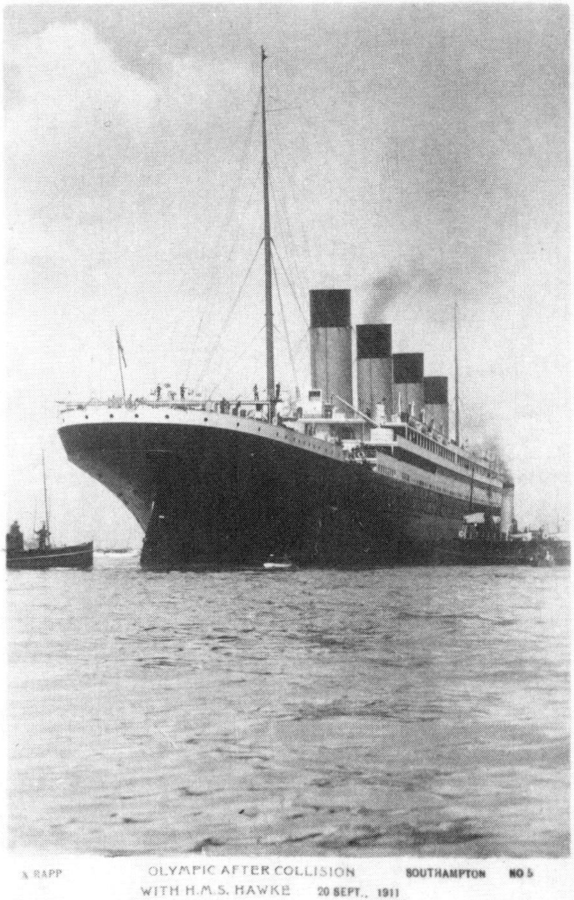

THE COLLISION BETWEEN THE 'OLYMPIC' AND H.M.S. 'HAWKE'

During the forenoon of 20th September, 1911, 'Olympic' set out on her fifth voyage from Southampton under the command of Capt. E. J. Smith. As the ship rounded Calshot Spit, negotiating the difficult reverse S-turn known as the Bramble, to turn into Spithead and travelling at moderate speed, a cruiser H.M.S. 'Hawke' was sighted coming up the Solent three miles away.

The alteration of course by the 'Olympic' to turn into Spithead caused the two ships to become parallel with each other and at a distance of 100 – 300 yards apart.

Suddenly the 'Hawke' altered to port to pass astern of the liner and during this action, a collision occured with the 'Hawke' hitting the 'Olympic' 80 feet from the stern, on the Starboard quarter. The 'Hawke's' bows were badly damaged, with the collision causing a 40 feet long gash on the 'Olympic'.

The 'Olympic's' passengers were disembarked at Cowes and the postcard shows the ship returning to Southampton for inspection.

(Published by A. Rapp, Southampton – M. Bown collection)

THE COLLISION BETWEEN THE 'OLYMPIC' AND H.M.S. 'HAWKE'

At the collision inquiry, the Admiralty gave evidence that the liner had crowded the channel, the 'Hawke's' helm had jammed and the cruiser had been drawn in towards the liner, through the suction caused by the difference in displacements of the two vessels. The inquiry found the 'Olympic' to blame, with no blame attached to the White Star Line, because the liner was being piloted. An appeal was made, but both The Court of Appeal and the House of Lords upheld the ruling.

The illustration shows a closer view of the damage to the 'Olympic's' hull.

(Published by A. Rapp, Southampton – M. Bown collection)

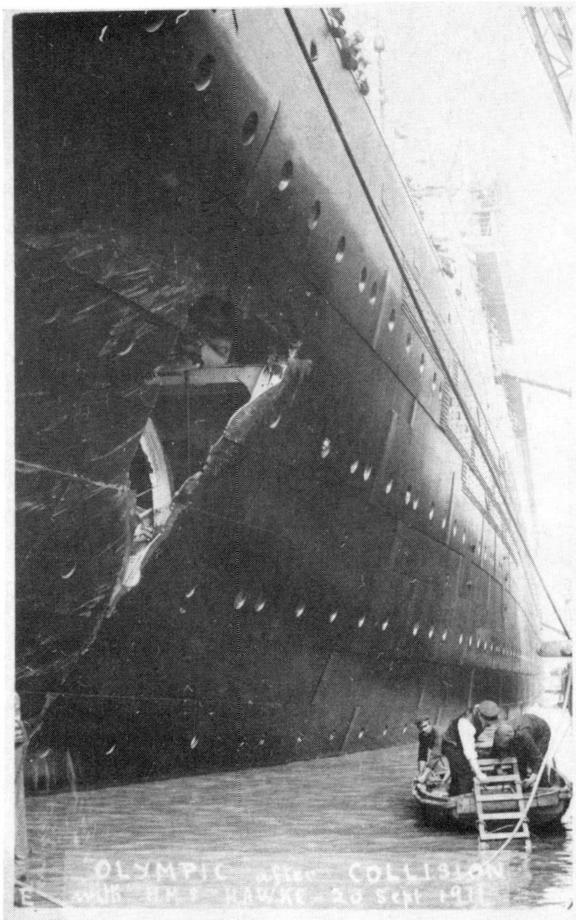

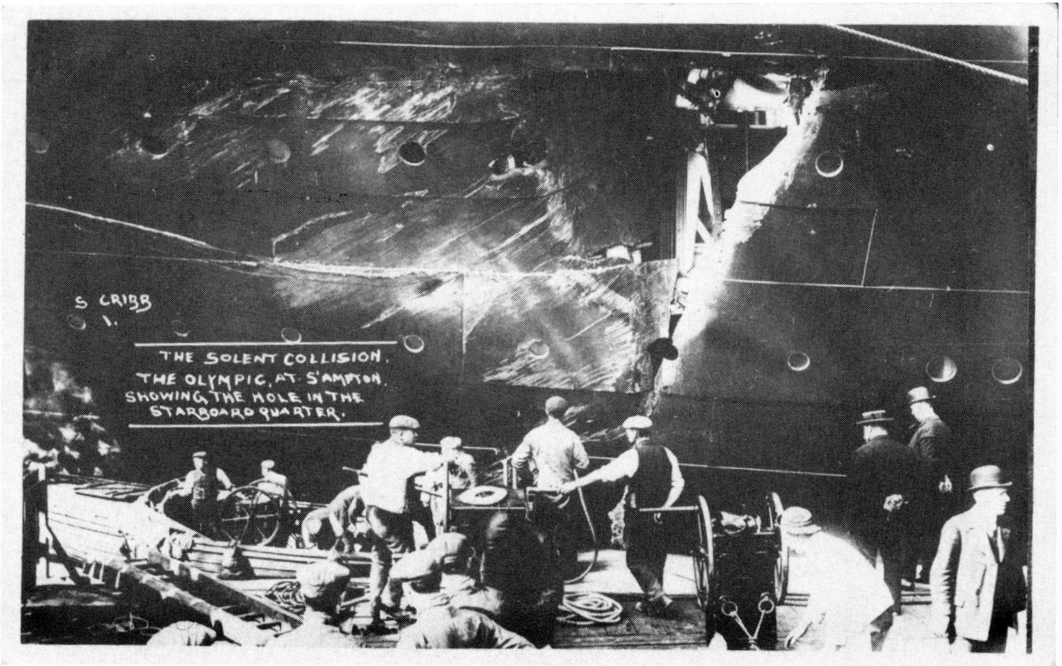

THE COLLISION BETWEEN THE 'OLYMPIC' AND H.M.S. 'HAWKE'

A further view of the gaping hole and buckled plates with officials and workers inspecting the damage in Southampton Dock.

The postcard was posted on 29th September, 1911 with the message "Saw this boat in docks, she has an enormous hole in the back".

The 'Olympic' returned to Belfast under reduced speed for immediate repairs. She was dry docked on 6th October for six weeks with shipyard workers being transferred from the 'Titanic' to quickly complete the repairs.

(Published by S. Cribb – M. Bown collection)

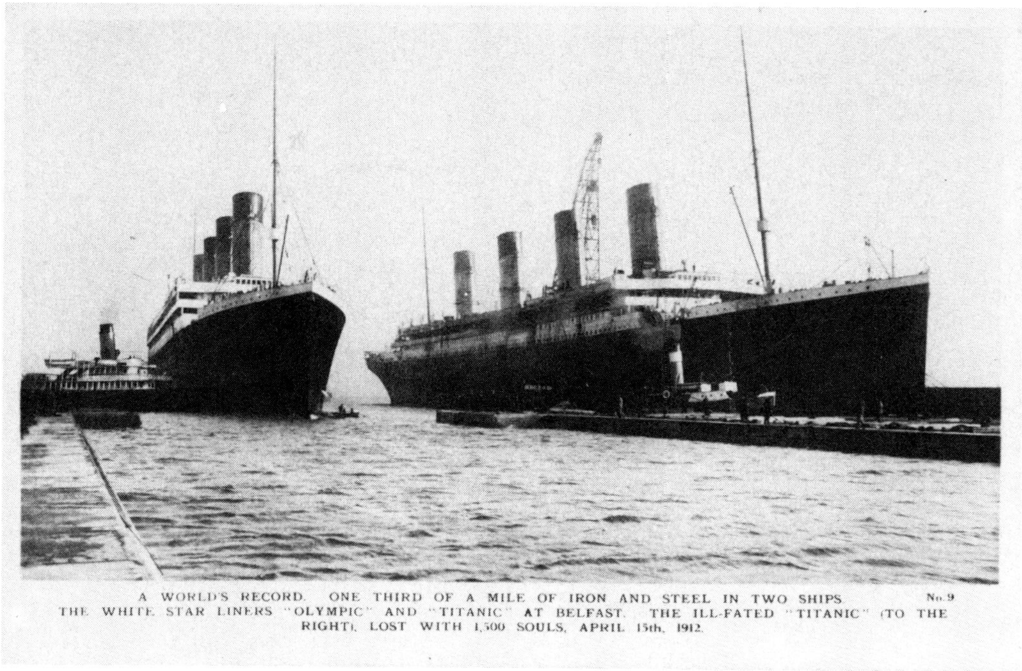

THE 'OLYMPIC' AND 'TITANIC' AT BELFAST

On 24th February, 1912, the 'Olympic' lost a propeller blade while crossing the Atlantic on her way to Southampton, and was once again returned to Belfast for repairs.
The 'Titanic' meanwhile was nearing her final completion and had to vacate the Thompson graving dock, as it was the only dry dock big enough to fit the liner for its repairs.
The postcard shows the 'Olympic' being edged into the dry dock for her propeller blade to be replaced on 6th March, 1912.

(Published by Walton, Belfast – M. Bown collection)

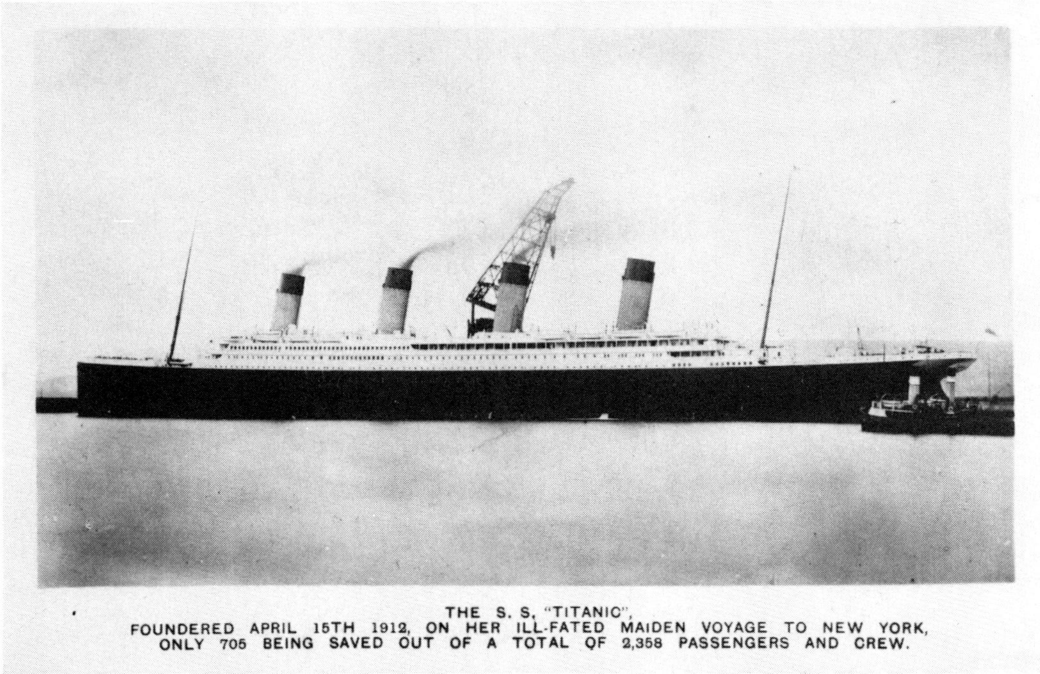

SEA TRIALS, BELFAST

One month before completion the 'Titanic' had an additional feature made that was to distinguish her from the 'Olympic'. The forward half of the promenade deck was plated and enclosed with windows, to protect the passengers from sea spray.

Ten months after the launch, the 'Titanic' was finally completed, sea trials were scheduled for 1st April, 1912, but due to strong north-west winds, the trials were postponed.

The illustration shows the 'Titanic' preparing for trials on 1st April. Note how the wind curls the smoke from her funnels. Behind the third funnel, can be seen the giant 200-ton floating crane, used to lift the machinery on board during the fitting out.

(Published by Hurst & Co., Belfast – M. Bown collection)

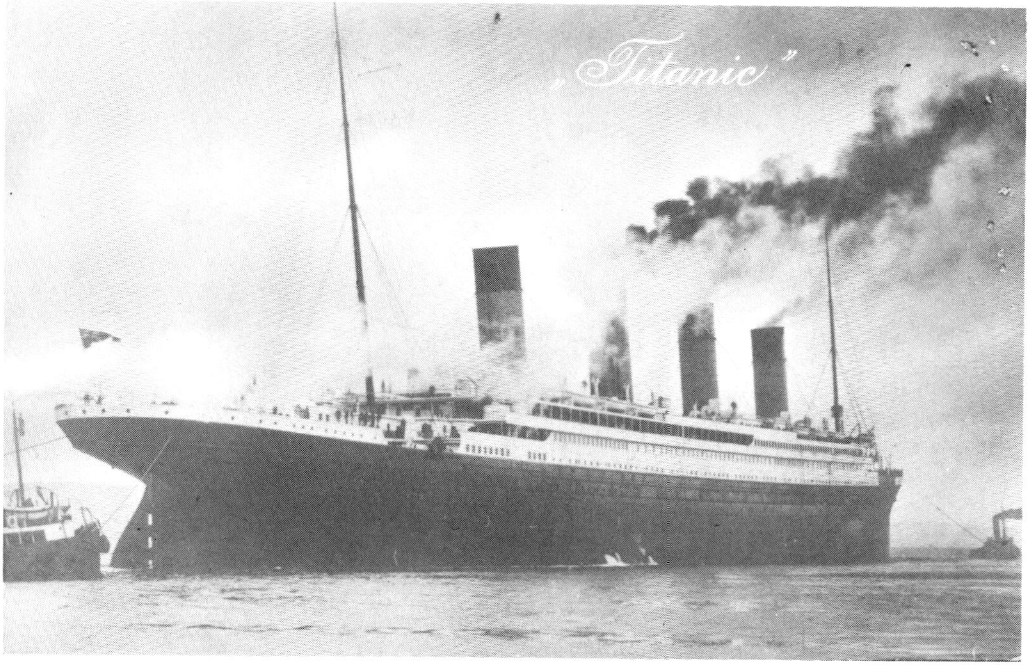

SEA TRIALS, BELFAST

At 6 a.m. on 2nd April, 1912, five tugs were attached to the 'Titanic' and guided her down Victoria Channel to Belfast Lough. The postcard produced by a German publisher, shows the 'Titanic' shortly before the tugs cast off and commencing her trials under her own power. The trials included manoeuvring the vessel at different speeds, testing the effectiveness of her helm and conducting an emergency stop, which took the ship just less than half a mile to come to rest after travelling at 20 knots.

The 'Titanic' returned to Belfast Lough by 7 p.m. She received her passenger certificate after the successful completion of the trials and disembarked the observers from Harland and Wolff.

(M. Bown collection)

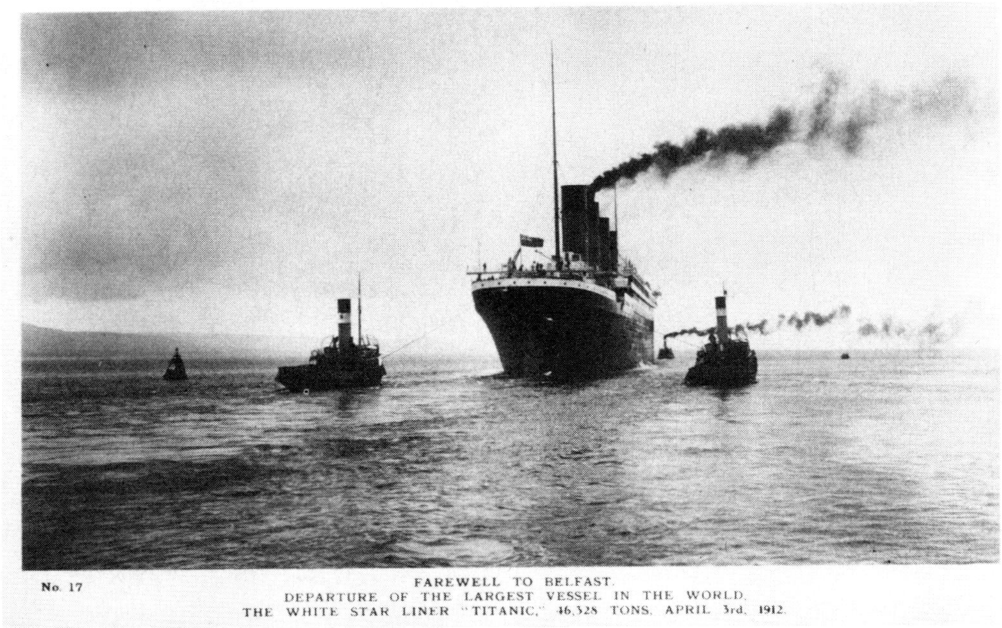

DEPARTURE FROM BELFAST

Under the command of Capt. E. J. Smith, who had earlier transferred from the 'Olympic', the 'Titanic' left Belfast at 8 p.m. on the same day of her trials and commenced the voyage down the Irish Sea and St. George's Channel, around Land's End into the English Channel and up to Southampton. The postcard shows a further view of the 'Titanic' being guided and towed into Belfast Lough before her trials, by the tugs 'Huskisson' and 'Herculaneum' at her stern and 'Hornby' on her starboard bow. The tugs 'Hercules' and 'Herald' are hidden from view.

(Published by Walton, Belfast – R. Simmons collection)

ARRIVAL AT SOUTHAMPTON

The 'Titanic' arrived at Southampton late in the evening of 3rd April, and just after midnight docked at Berth 44.

On Thursday, 4th April, preparations began to load the ship and prepare it for its maiden voyage.

The following day was Good Friday and the postcard shows the 'Titanic' at her best, dressed overall in flags for the benefit of the people of Southampton.

Many came to view her from the harbour or from an excursion steamer.

None of the general public were allowed on board.

(Published by H. Symes, Southampton – R. Simmons collection)

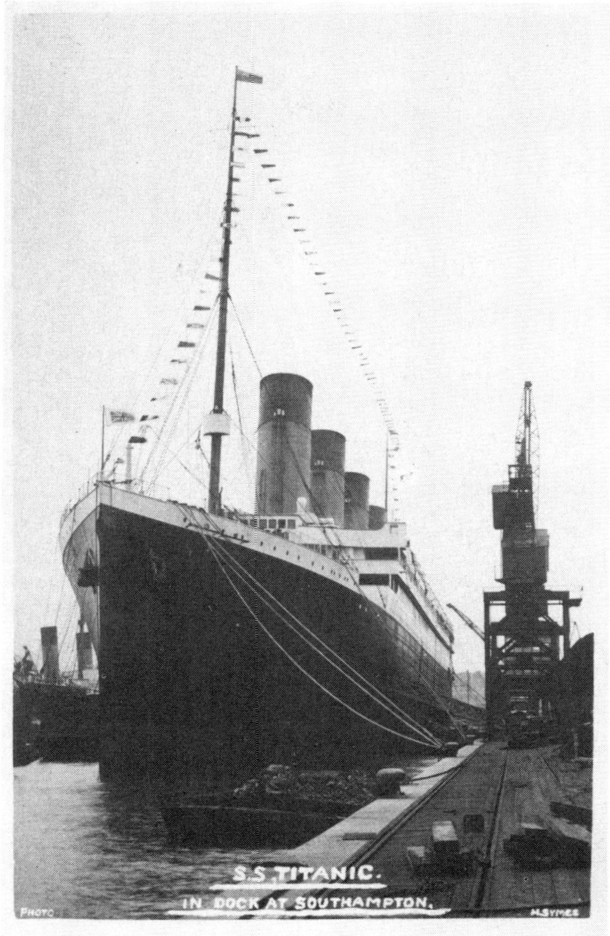

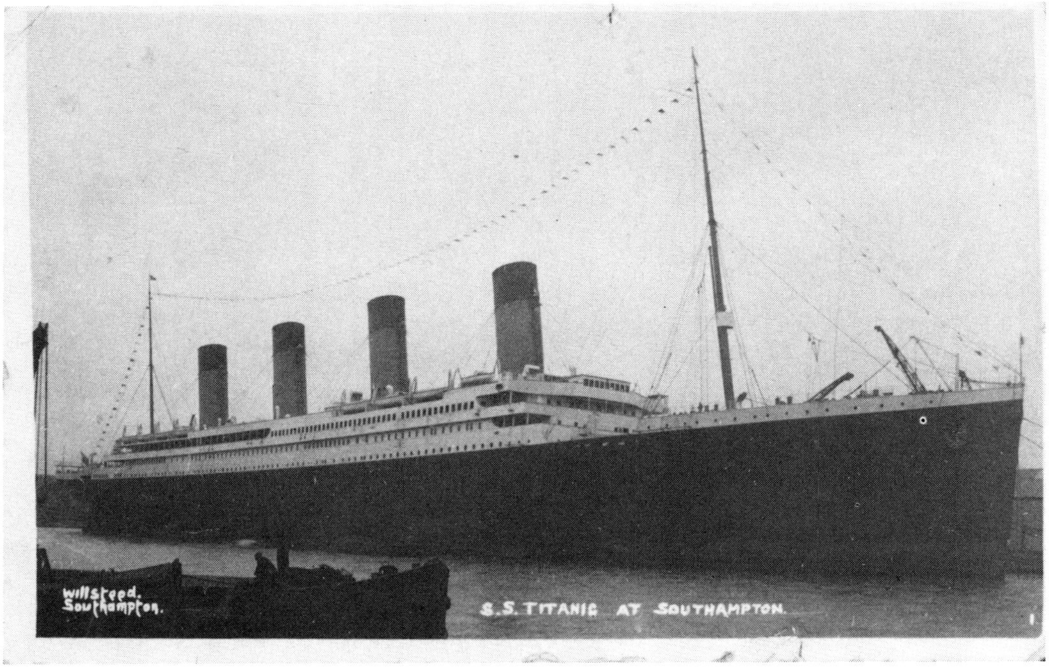

PREPARATIONS AT SOUTHAMPTON

There had been a coal strike in the country since January, 1912 and this was finally settled on 6th April, 1912. The shortage of coal, resulted in the 'Titanic' being fuelled by coal taken from five other company owned ships that were docked at Southampton.

The coal strike had also caused widespread unemployment in Southampton and on Saturday, 6th April, the majority of the crew were recruited.

(Also photographed on Good Friday, 5th April, 1912 and published by Willsteed, Southampton – M. Bown collection)

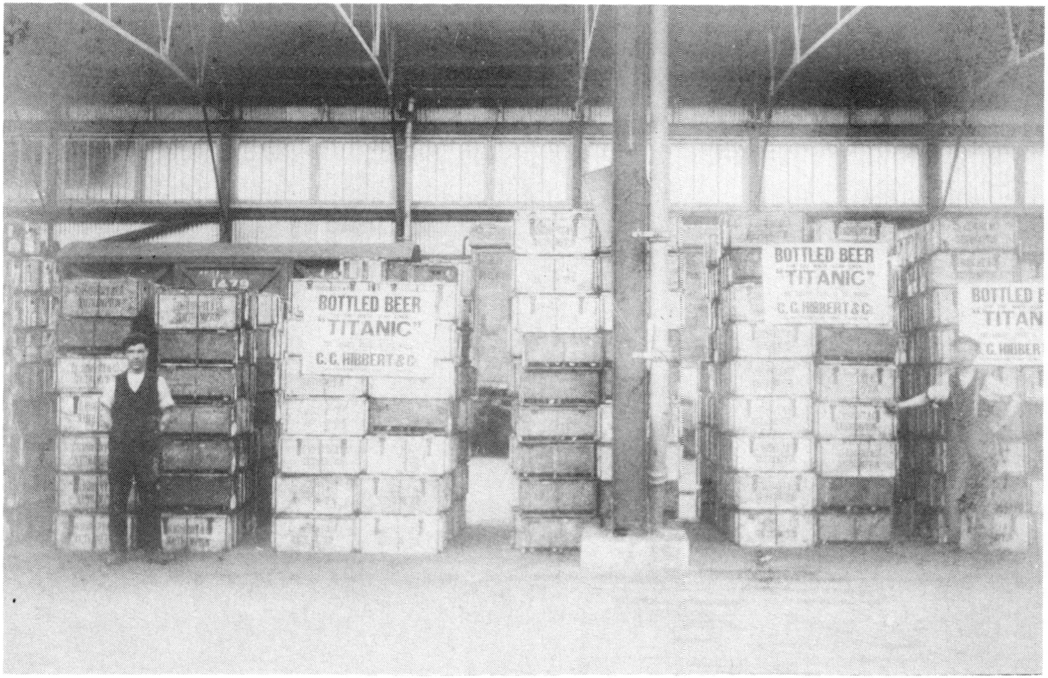

LOADING STORES AT SOUTHAMPTON

A very rare postcard showing part of the consignment of 15,000 bottles of beer,
about to be loaded on board the 'Titanic'.
The notices read, "Bottled Beer for the White Star liner, TITANIC. The largest vessel in the World.
C. G. Hibbert & Co., Southampton and London."

(M. Bown collection)

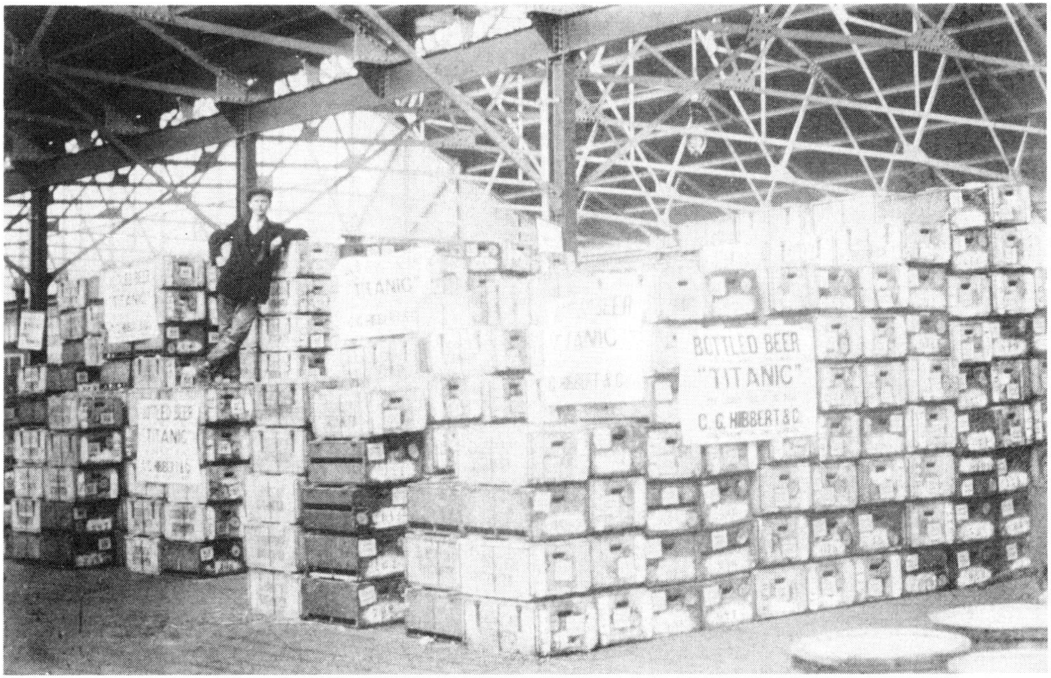

LOADING STORES AT SOUTHAMPTON

A further view of the vast beer stocks prior to loading.
The 'Titanic' also loaded the following supplies and catering equipment:

Fresh Meat	75,000 lbs.	Flour	250 barrels	Sugar	5 tons	Electroplate	26,000 pieces
Poultry	25,000 lbs.	Tea	1,000 lbs.	Potatoes	40 tons	Crockery	46,000 pieces
Fresh Eggs	35,000	Fresh Milk	1,500 gals.	Minerals	12,000 bottles	Glass	7,000 pieces
Cereals	10,000 lbs.	Fresh Cream	300 gals.	Wines	1,000 bottles	Cutlery	5,000 pieces

A wide variety of general cargo of all descriptions and weighing 559 tons was also loaded.

(M. Bown collection)

CAPTAIN EDWARD JOHN SMITH, R.D., R.N.R.

Edward (Teddy) John Smith was born on 27th January, 1850 in Hanley, Stoke-on-Trent, Staffordshire. He was educated at Hanley and Etruria British Schools. After leaving school he joined the Merchant Navy and joined the White Star Line in 1880, taking his first command of the steamship 'Republic' in 1887.

His other earlier commands included 'Britannic', 'Germanic', 'Majestic' and the 'Baltic', his tenth command.

Capt. Smith was White Star's senior Captain and also the highest paid, serving on the North Atlantic service. He was appointed Master of the 'Olympic' for its maiden voyage in June, 1911 and transferred to the 'Titanic' to join the ship in Belfast for its trials and preparations for the maiden voyage at the beginning of April, 1912.

He was shortly due to retire and his appointment to the 'Titanic' was considered the height of his career.

(M. Bown collection)

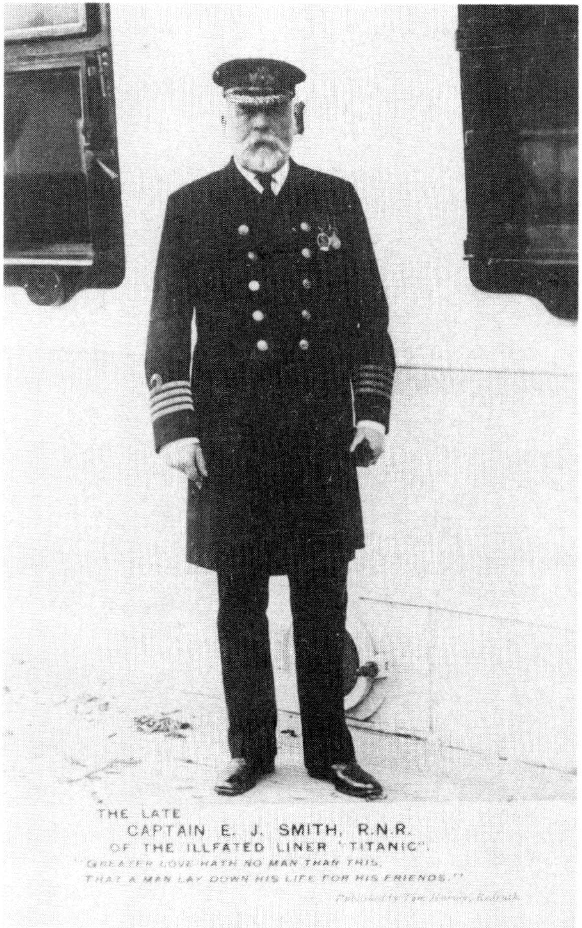

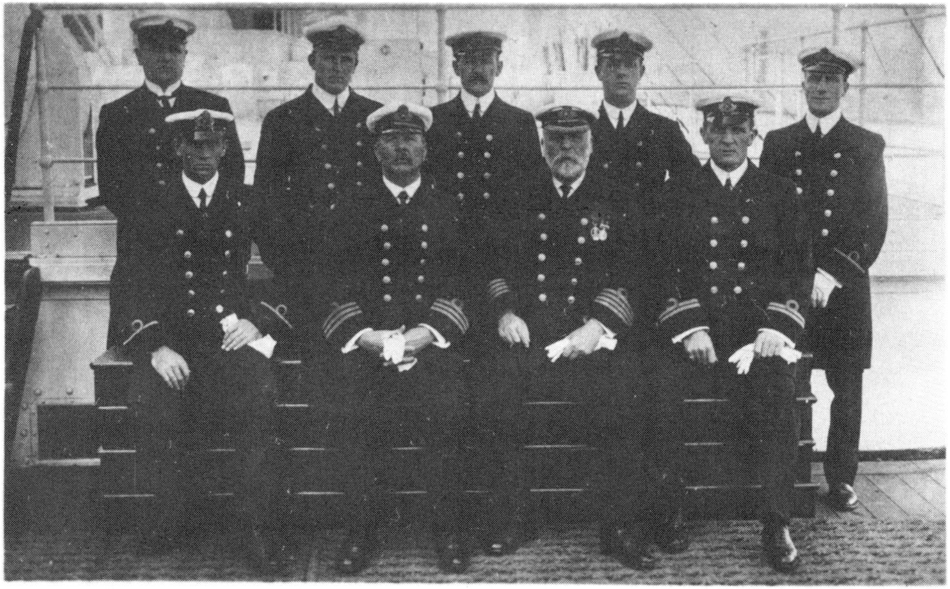

CAPTAIN SMITH, & OFFICERS OF THE TITANIC.

CAPTAIN SMITH AND DECK OFFICERS OF THE 'TITANIC'

Photographed on board 'Titanic' prior to the maiden voyage from Southampton. Standing from left to right: Herbert W. McElroy, Chief Purser; Charles H. Lightoller, Second Officer, (Survived); Herbert J. Pitman, Third Officer, (Survived); Joseph G. Boxall, Fourth Officer, (Survived); Harold G. Lowe, Fifth Officer, (Survived).
Seated from left to right:
James P. Moody, Sixth Officer; Henry T. Wilde, Chief Officer; Captain Edward John Smith, R.D., R.N.R.; William M. Murdock, First Officer, (who was on the bridge at the time the 'Titanic' struck the iceberg).

(Published by Signal in their Real Photographic Series – M. Bown collection)

AT SOUTHAMPTON

An unusual photograph reproduced on a postcard, showing the third and fourth funnels and the centre section of the 'Titanic'. The fourth or 'dummy' funnel was used for ventilation purposes only and it is interesting to note how many pictures of the 'Titanic' show the liner with smoke issuing from all four funnels.
On the reverse of the postcard, the message reads: " 'Titanic' with Fred's yacht alongside just prior to departure from Southampton".

(Publisher unknown – M. Bown collection)

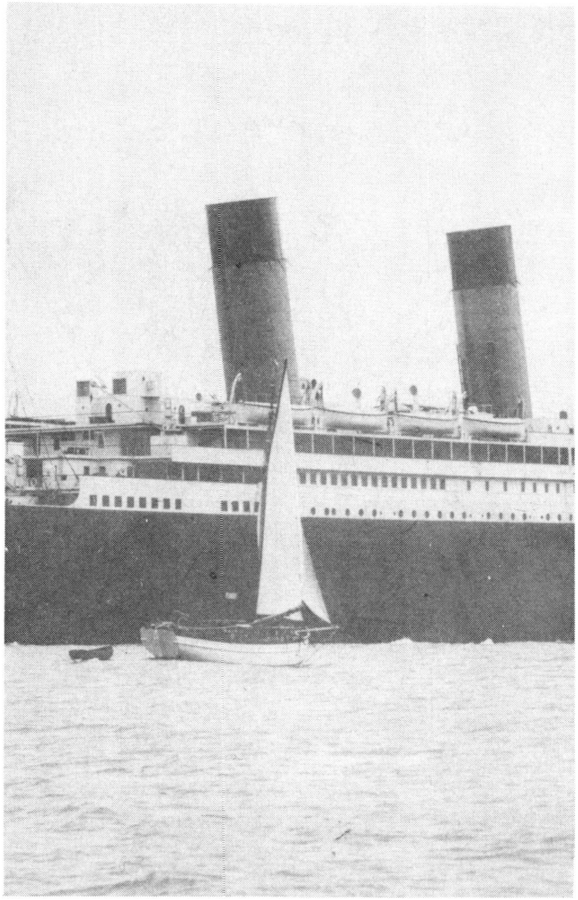

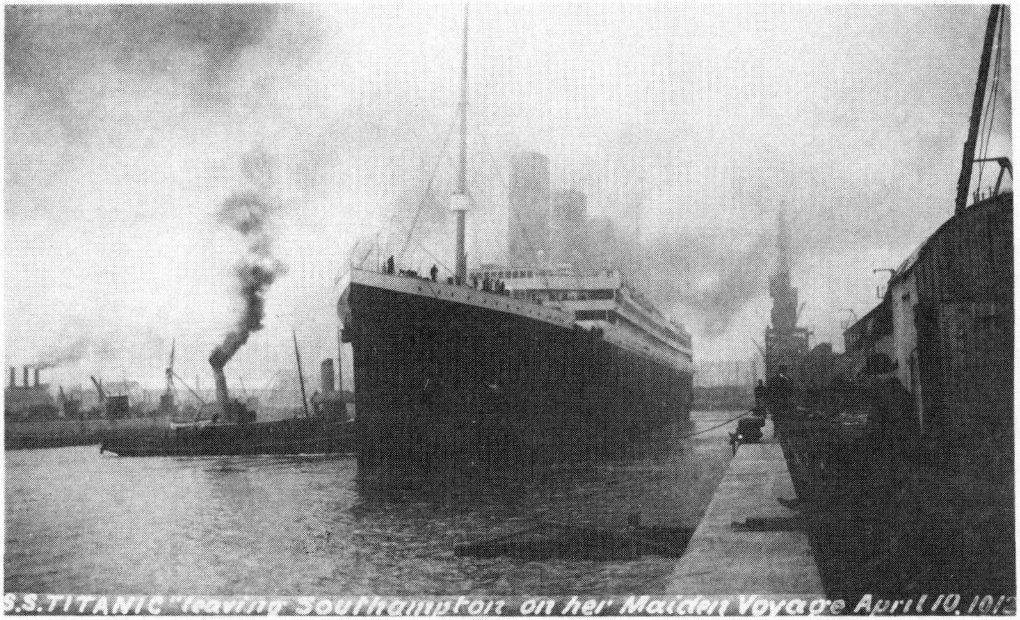

DEPARTURE FROM SOUTHAMPTON

By early Wednesday morning, 10th April, 1912 all the crew had been mustered on board and made final preparations checking equipment and passengers lists. The complement of officers and crew totalled 898 men and women. Later the same morning, the boat trains arrived at the dockside with 180 first-class, 240 second-class and 494 third-class passengers joining the 'Titanic' for its maiden voyage.
At just after 12 noon, the 'Titanic' cast off from Berth 44, piloted by George Bowyer and assisted by six tugs.

(Published in a series by G. D. Courtney, Photographer, Southampton – R. Simmons collection)

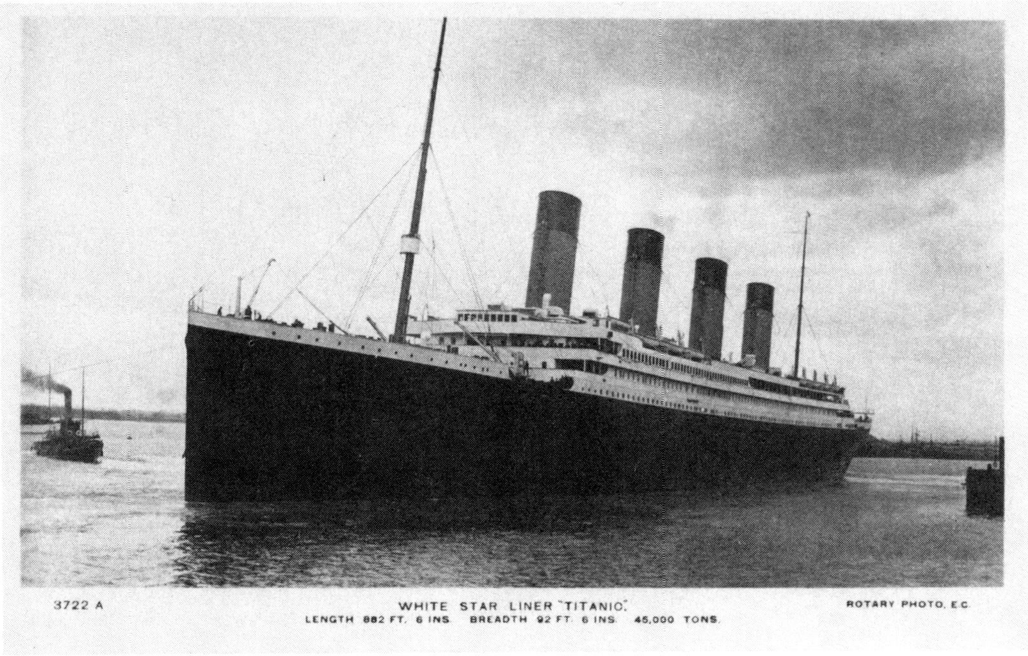

DEPARTURE FROM SOUTHAMPTON

Among the 914 passengers on board were many famous people. These included Mr. Bruce Ismay, Chairman of White Star and Mr. Thomas Andrews, Managing Director of Harland and Wolff, with eight representatives from the shipyard.

There were no fewer than ten millionaires, whose combined capital totalled £120,000,000. In the company of this elite group were Colonel J. J. Astor and his wife, both belonging to one of the wealthiest families in the world. Other notable passengers were the Countess of Rothes, many industrialists, bankers and even honeymoon couples. The illustration shows the 'Titanic' being towed away from her berth. Two varieties are known to exist of this postcard, with the more common variety giving details of the disaster.

(Published by Rotary Photographic Company – M. Bown collection)

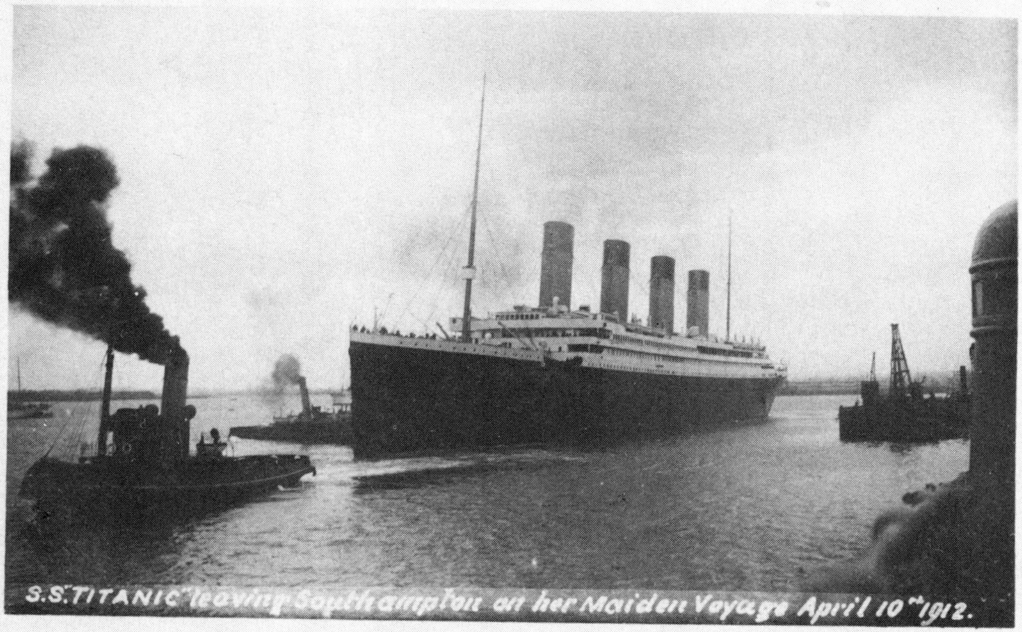

DEPARTURE FROM SOUTHAMPTON

As the 'Titanic' proceeded down the River Test, she aproached the two liners 'Oceanic' and 'New York' moored in tandem at Berth 38. The turbulence caused by the propellers and the variation of water displacement from the passing 'Titanic' resulted in a tremendous strain on the ropes, securing both ships. The ropes on the 'Oceanic' held but those holding the 'New York' snapped and the liner broke away from her mooringss and started to swing sternwards in an arc towards the 'Titanic'. The 'Titanic' was put astern and the resultant flow of water was sufficient to halt the 'New York' within twelve feet of her stern. The 'New York' was secured to a tug and towed and moored downstream. This incident delayed her departure for an hour and when all was clear, the 'Titanic' once again proceeded towards Southampton Water.

(Published in the series by G. D. Courtney, Southampton – M. Bown collection)

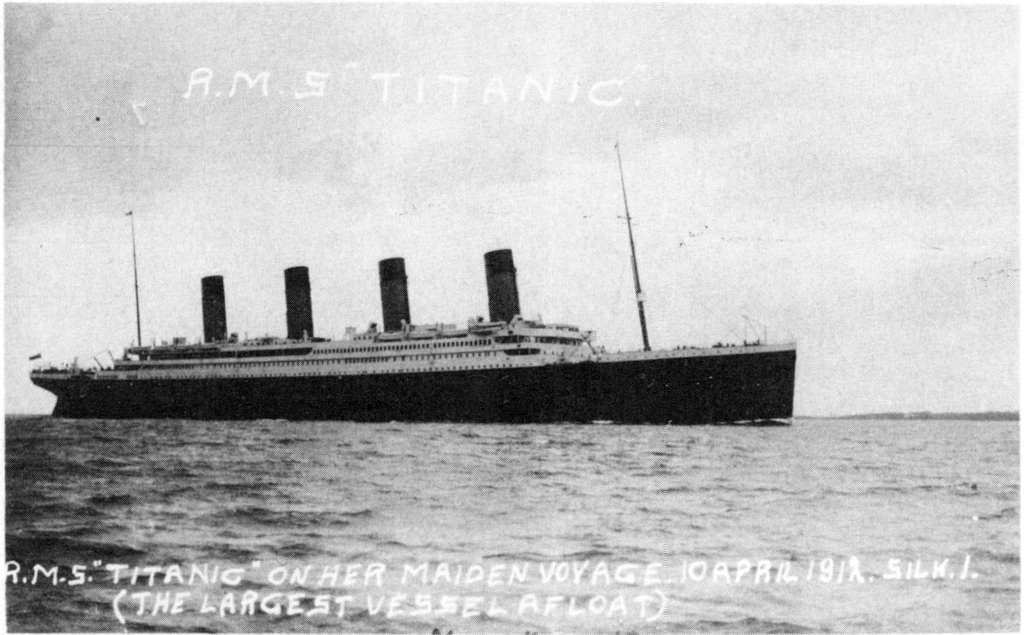

DEPARTURE FROM SOUTHAMPTON

A rare postcard postally used on 7th May, 1912, illustrating the 'Titanic' under way in Southampton Water. The postcard has an interesting message on its reverse:

"This is the photo I promised you, taken as she is going around the corner at Ryde heading straight away for Cherbourg. You will see the only difference between her and the 'Olympic' is her top deck, covered in back to her third funnel. She is three inches longer and a trifle wider to make the extra 1000 tons (46,000) against the 'Olympic's' (45,000)".

(Published by Reginald Silk, Portsmouth – M. Bown collection)

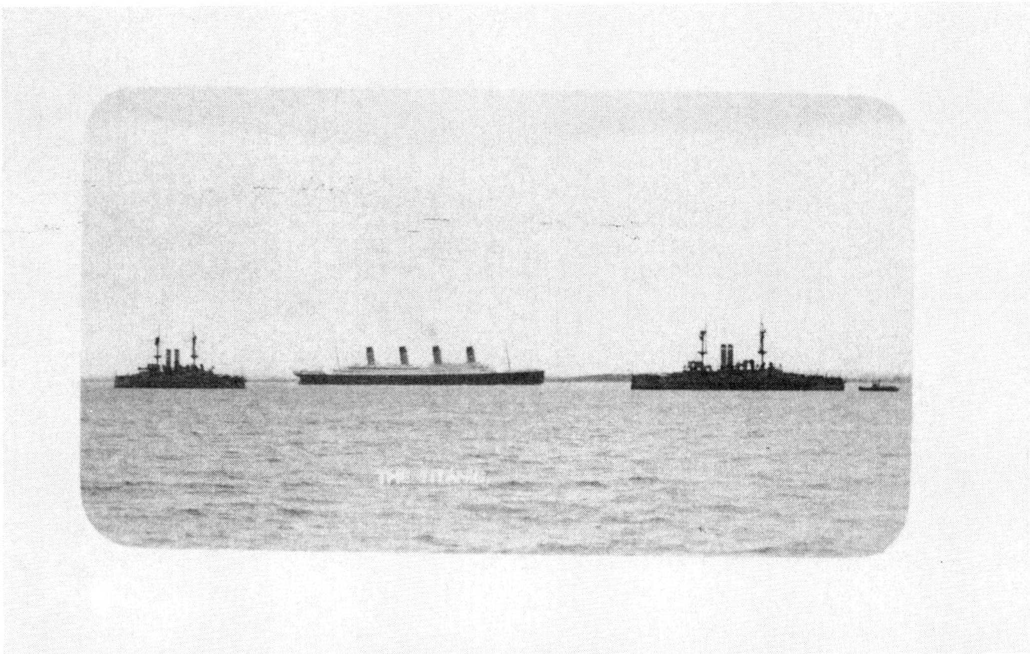

DEPARTURE FROM SOUTHAMPTON

A distant photograph of the 'Titanic' passing between two destroyers at the naval anchorage in Spithead. Laurence Beesley, a second-class passenger and a teacher from Dulwich College, London noted that the ship had earlier exchanged salutes with one of the White Star tugs waiting for one of the White Star liners homeward bound. Close to the Nab lightship, the 'Titanic' reduced her speed, which allowed the waiting pilot cutter to collect the pilot, George Bowyer. The liner then made her way across the English Channel to Cherbourg.

(Published by W. R. Hogg, Ryde – R. Simmons collection)

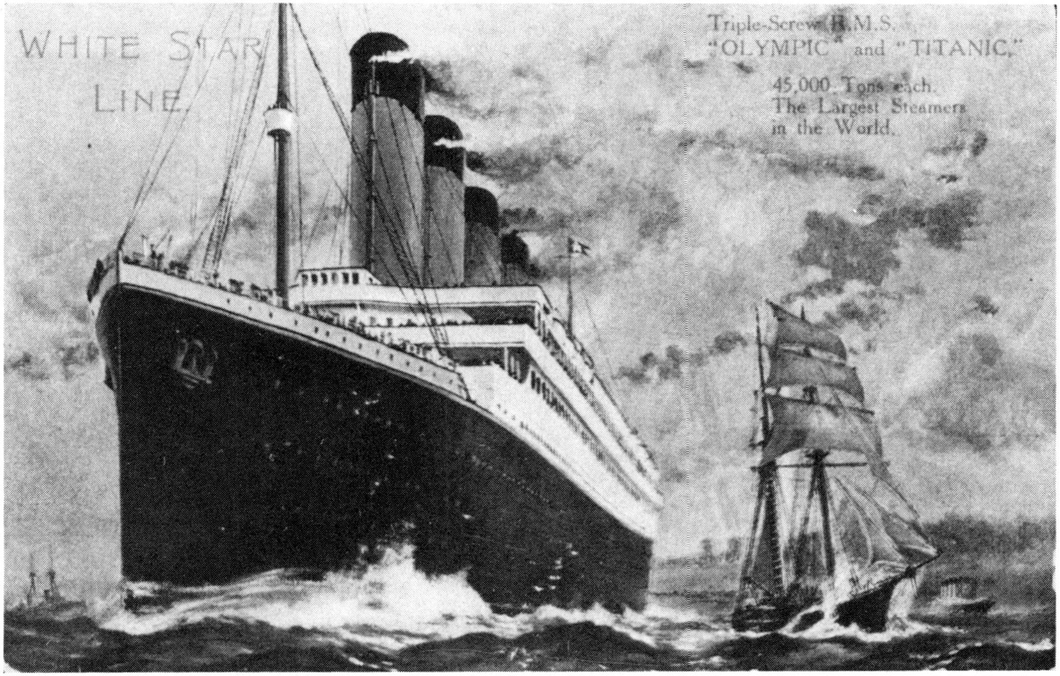

CHERBOURG

The 'Titanic' arrived at Cherbourg and anchored close to the harbour at 6.30 p.m., 10th April. Two White Star tenders, 'Nomadic' and 'Traffic' ferried 274 passengers (142 first-class, 30 second-class and 102 third-class) and additional bags of mail out to the waiting liner.

Many of the first-class 'society' passengers had just finished the 'Season' in Europe, and among them was the millionaire, Mr. B. Guggenheim. At 8 p.m. the tenders returned to harbour and the 'Titanic' weighed anchor and set course for Queenstown in Southern Ireland.

The White Star watercolour postcard illustrated above would have been freely available on board and many would have been mailed by passengers from Cherbourg or Queenstown.

(M. Bown collection)

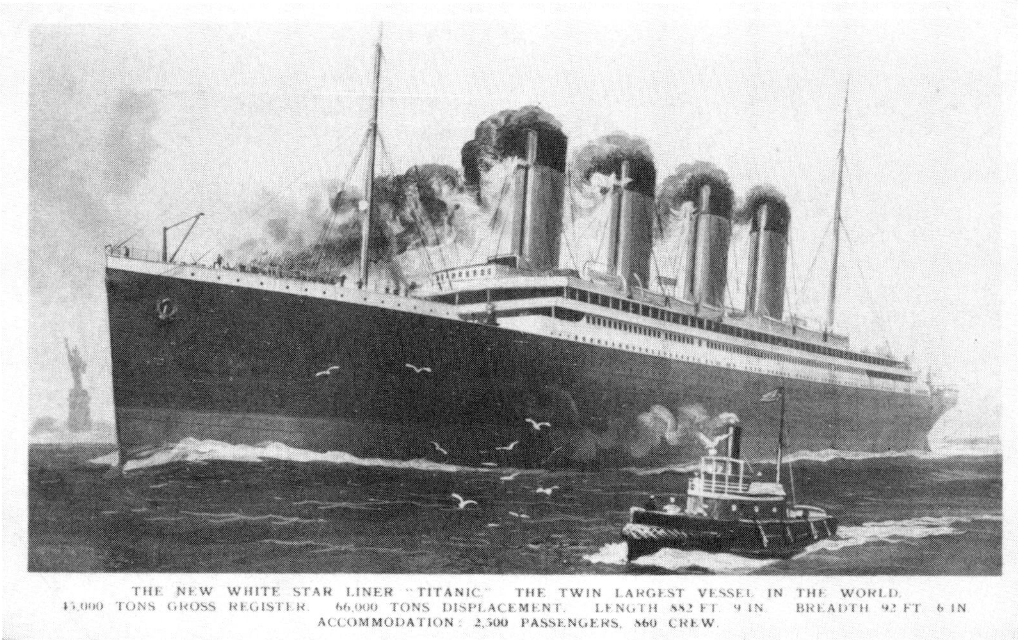

QUEENSTOWN

The passage to Queenstown took twenty hours and the 'Titanic' anchored two miles offshore at 11.30 a.m. on Thursday, 11th April. 120 passengers (7 second-class and 113 third class) and further bags of mail were ferried out by the tenders, 'America' and 'Ireland'. Many of the passengers were emigrants to America.
At 1.30 p.m. the liner weighed anchor and departed from Queenstown for New York.
The total passenger complement of 1,308 now included 322 first-class, 277 second-class and 709 third-class passengers.

(An artist drawn postcard of the 'Olympic' but entitled 'Titanic', published by Walton, Belfast.
Note the Statue of Liberty on the left. – M. Bown collection)

THE LOSS OF THE 'TITANIC'

Throughout Sunday, 14th April, the radio room, manned by Jack Phillips and his assistant, Harold Bride, had received and reported many warnings about the existence of an extensive field of pack ice and icebergs that had drifted south into the main shipping lanes. By the evening, the air temperature had fallen to 31°F and the ship's carpenter was instructed to watch that the fresh water tanks did not freeze.

The night was clear and with good visibility the ship maintained a speed of 22 knots. Just after 11.30 p.m. the look-out in the crow's nest sounded a warning of three bells and phoned the bridge with the message, "Iceberg, right ahead".

(Publisher unknown: note how the postcard has been reconstructed from the original H. Symes photograph taken on 5th April, while at Southampton. (see page 31). – R. Simmons collection)

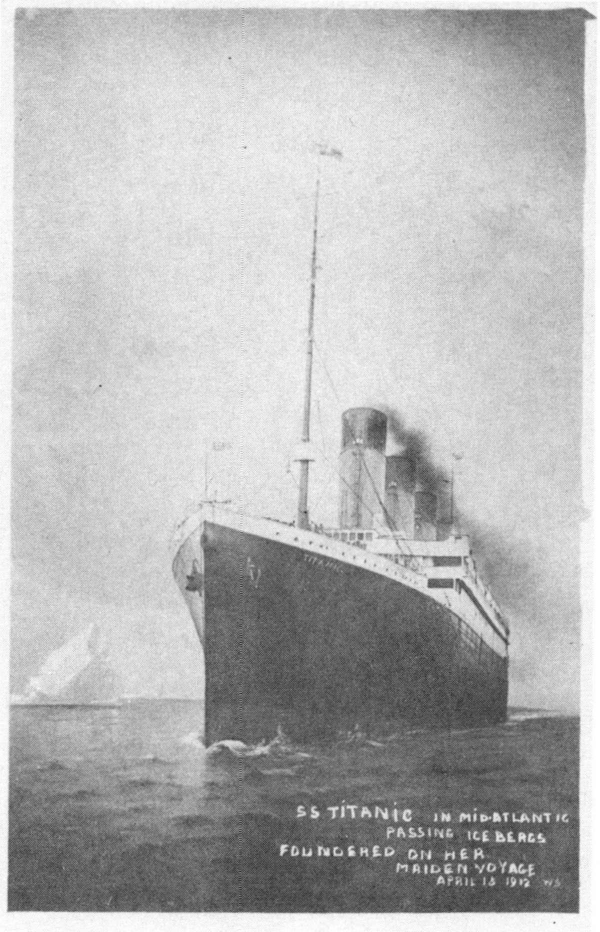

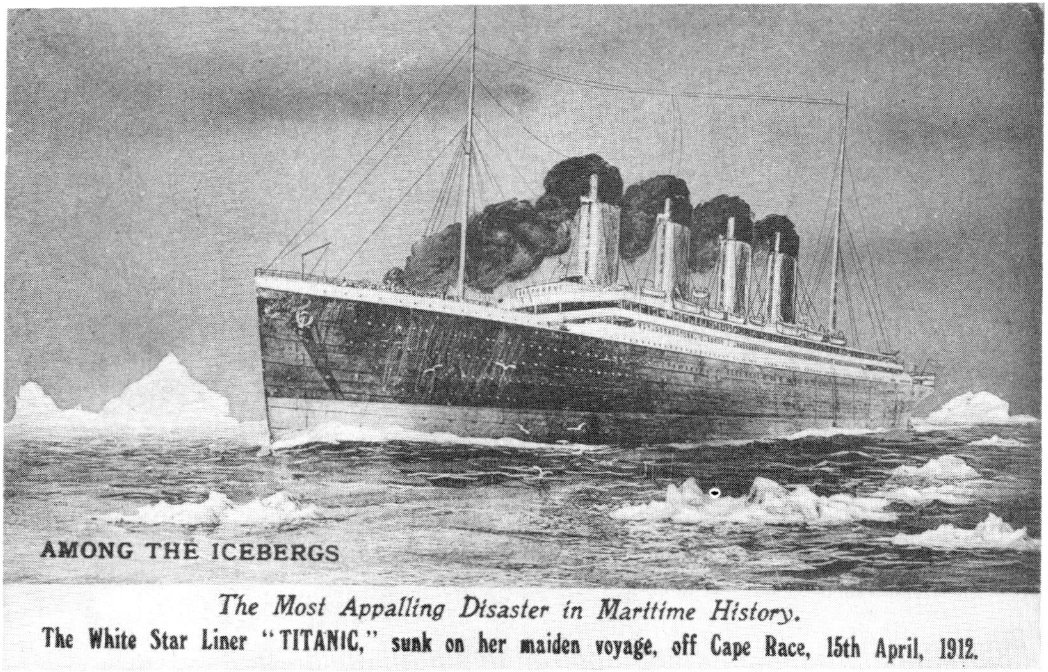

THE LOSS OF THE 'TITANIC'

First Officer Murdoch on duty on the bridge immediately ordered 'Full Astern', 'Hard-a-starboard' and closed the watertight doors. This prompt action prevented a direct collision, but the iceberg struck the 'Titanic' below the waterline on its starboard side, buckling the plates and opening the seams. Water flooded in along a three hundred feet gash extending from number one hold to number six boiler room. Captain Smith appeared on the bridge and with Thomas Andrews calculated that the ship would not last much longer than two hours.

Fourth Officer Boxall meanwhile calculated that the ship's postion was 41° 46′ N, 50° 14′ W.

At 12.05 a.m., Captain Smith gave the order to uncover the boats and assemble crew and passengers.

(Published by Valentines – R. Simmons collection)

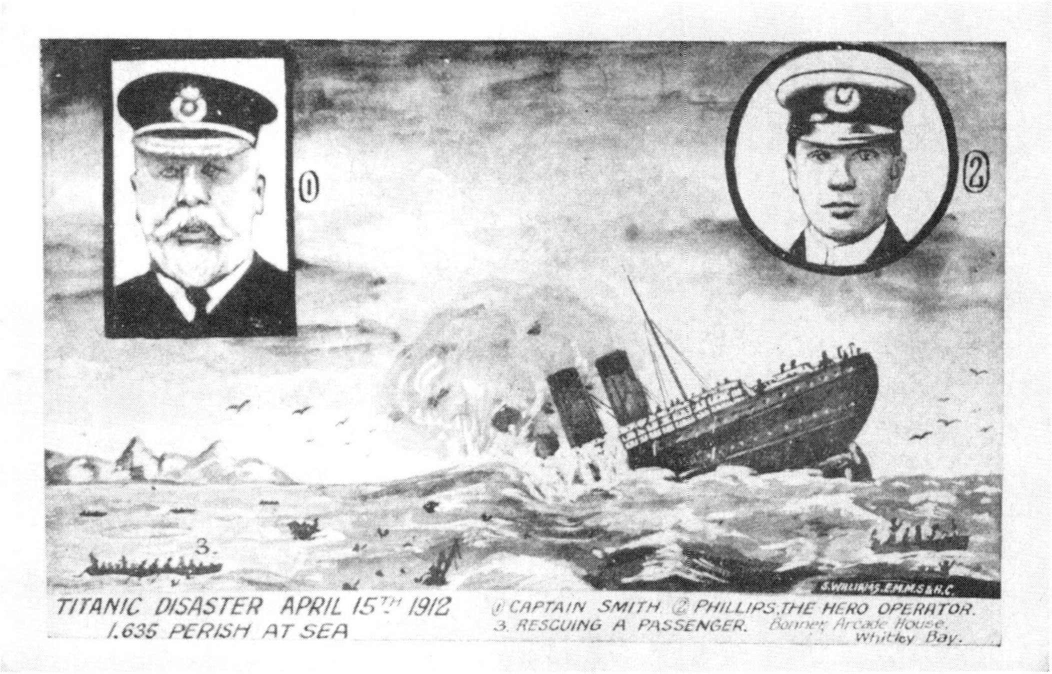

THE LOSS OF THE 'TITANIC'

Captain Smith took the calculated ship's position to the radio operator, Jack Phillips, who transmitted the distress signal, C.Q.D. at 12.15 a.m.. At 12.25 a.m. the Cunard owned 'Carpathia', which was fifty eight miles away to the south-east, answered the distress call and immediately altered course to the north-west, speeding at seventeen knots to assist the 'Titanic'. At the same time, the order was given to load the lifeboats. At 12.45 a.m. the first boat (number 7) was lowered, with less than half its capacity on board. Eight distress rockets were fired at five minute intervals from the bridge, who also noticed about six miles away the navigation lights of a mysterious vessel that appeared, turned and then vanished. Jack Phillips commenced using the new distress signal S.O.S. (The first time it was used by a passenger liner). Eleven ships heard 'Titanic's' signals but the majority were too far to render assistance quickly.

(Published by Bonner, Whitley Bay – M. Bown collection)

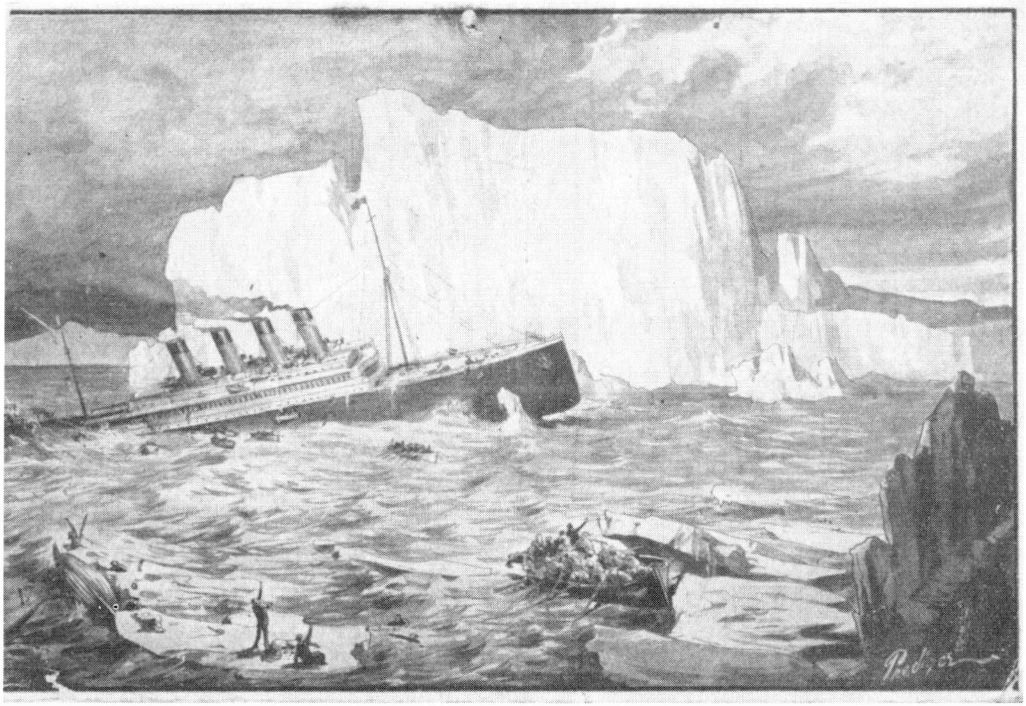

THE LOSS OF THE 'TITANIC'

Following the order that women and children were to have priority, there were many separations of husbands and wives. Many husbands had to force their wives into the boats, while some wives refused to leave their husbands. Many lifeboats were lowered without their full capacity and by 1.25 a.m, the remaining lifeboats were being overloaded. At 1.30 a.m., panic started by boat 14, resulting in Fifth Officer Lowe firing a revolver to control the passengers. By now the liner had settled well into the water and the last of the rigid lifeboats (number 4) was launched at 1.55 a.m.

(An unusual German published postcard by Oskar Stoltze, Hamburg. Note the size of the iceberg, the survivors on the small iceberg and the angle of the 'Titanic', sinking at the stern – R. Simmons collection)

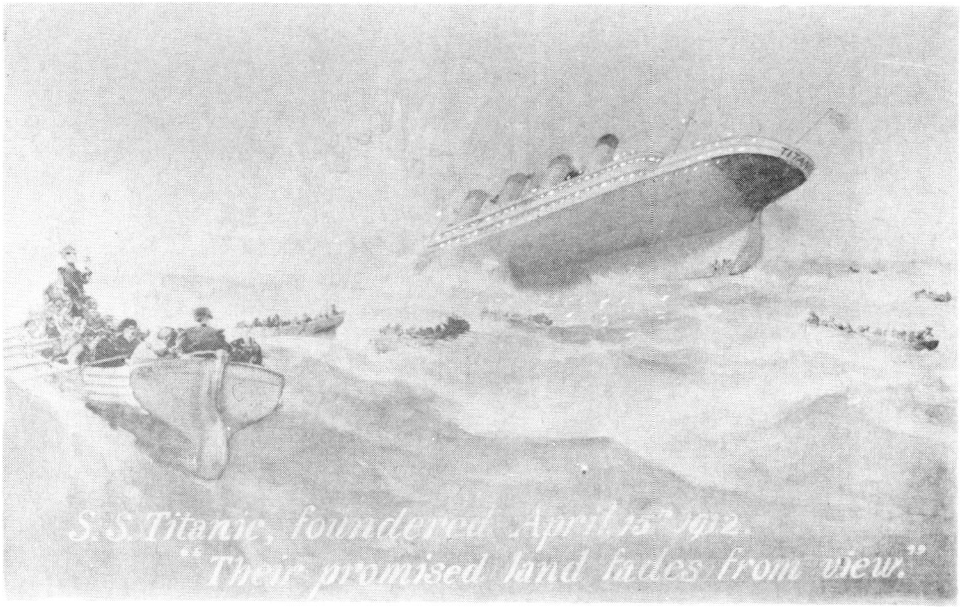

THE LOSS OF THE 'TITANIC'

Of the four remaining collapsible canvas lifeboats, 'C' and 'D' were launched successfully, with Bruce Ismay managing to escape in 'C' boat. Boats 'A' and 'B' became impossible to launch, but during the last moments were dislodged and managed to float away from the ship, upside down. At 2.05 a.m., Capt. Smith dismissed the two radio operators from their duties, but Phillips stayed on for a further fifteen minutes while there was enough power on board.

At 2.10 a.m., the bow became deeply submerged and the stern lifted above the water. As the angle rose towards the vertical, the forward funnel snapped from its mountings and a terrible roar was heard as all the moveable objects broke free and crashed downwards. By 2.20 a.m. the 'Titanic' had disappeared, plunging two miles down to the ocean floor.

(A dramatic artist impression of the last moments of the 'Titanic' with the caption: "Their promised land fades from view". Publisher unknown – M. Bown collection)

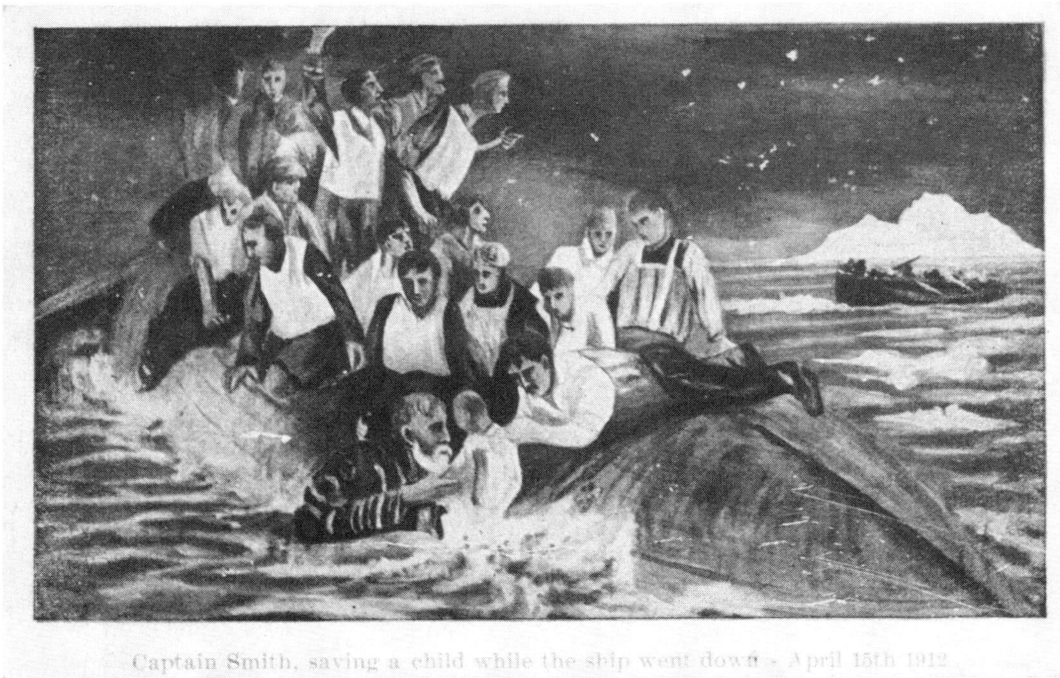

THE LOSS OF THE 'TITANIC'

There were many reports about what exactly happened to Captain Smith during the last moments of the ship. One report gave details that he had shot himself on the bridge, another report said that he had saved a child, as shown on the postcard, but there is little doubt that the true report of his death was that he died on the bridge alone, after doing his duty and having given his last order to the remaining passengers and crew, "Be British". The postcard also shows an artist's impression of the collapsible lifeboat 'A' being rescued by the lifeboat commanded by Fifth Officer Lowe.

(Published by White Star Publishing Company, New York – R. Simmons collection)

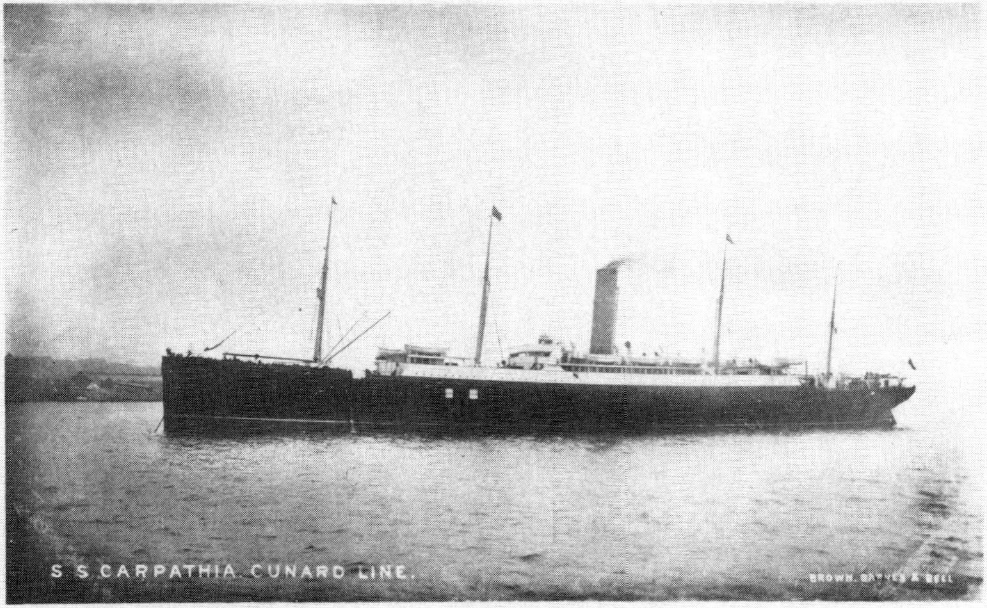

RESCUE BY THE 'CARPATHIA'

The 'Carpathia' commanded by Captain Rostron, arrived at the scene of the disaster just after 3.30 a.m.. By 8.30 a.m. after a thorough search all the survivors had been taken safely on board, and the ship proceeded to New York. Of the total of 2,206 passengers and crew, there were 703 survivors (493 passengers and 210 crew). At the same time, the 'Californian' commanded by Captain Lord and owned by the Leyland Line, arrived to assist the 'Carpathia' in searching for survivors. Later there was to be considerable controversy that the 'Californian' had been the mysterious ship sighted by the 'Titanic'. Capt. Lord always maintained that his ship had been stationary, surrounded by ice and having seen white rockets fired from a ship had tried unsuccessfully to contact it by Morse lamp.
The radio operator on the 'Californian' had been asleep all night, and had been unaware of the 'Titanic's' signals.
The 'Carpathia' finally arrived with the survivors in New York on Wednesday, 18th April.

(Published by Brown, Barnes & Bell – M. Bown collection)

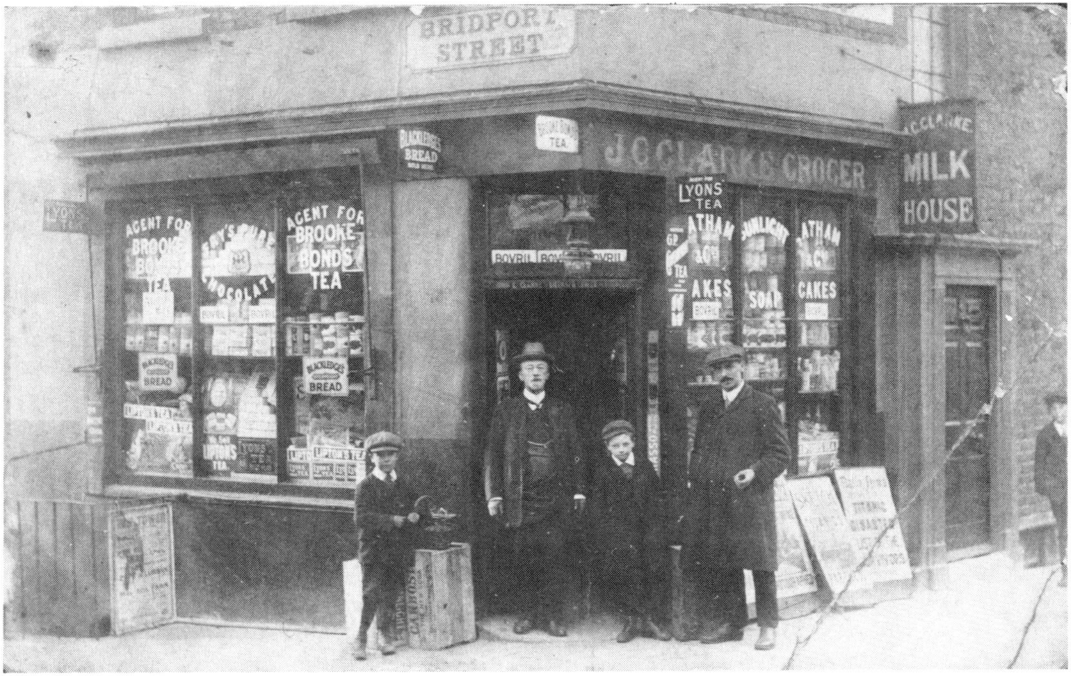

NEWSPAPER HEADLINES

When news reports were first received, the exact details of the disaster were confused, but by the evening of Tuesday, 16th April, the devastating news had been confirmed.

The first survivor lists were posted up on Wednesday, 17th April.

This photograph of J. C. Clarke's corner grocers shop, somewhere in north-west England, was taken shortly after the sinking of the 'Titanic'.

On the right of the picture the newspaper boards announce headlines from the Daily Sketch, 'TITANIC'S FAREWELL' and the Daily News, 'TITANIC' DISASTER – LIST OF THE SURVIVORS'.

(Publisher unknown – M. Bown collection)

JOE

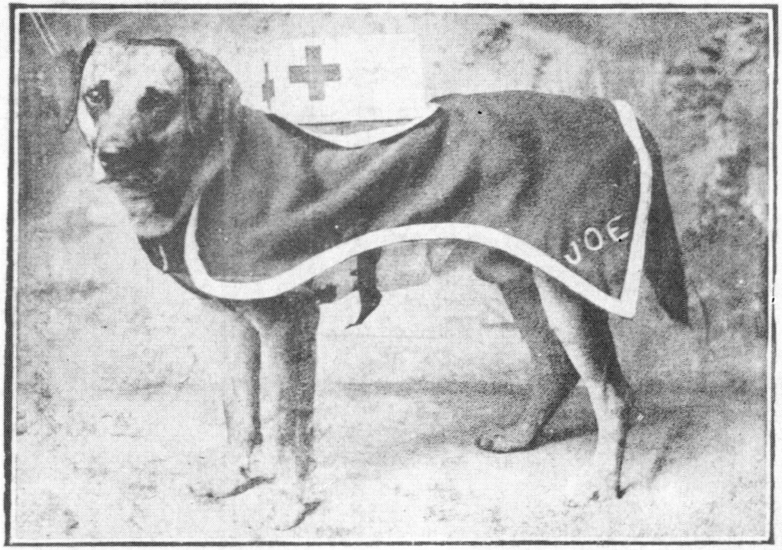

Who is endeavouring to collect £100 for the PRINCE OF WALES' HOSPITAL, TOTTENHAM. He was trained September, 1910, and was presented with a beautiful Silver Collar by the Earl of Malmesbury.

The sale of this Card is devoted to above.

He has also collected for the Help-the-Children Fund and the Convalescent Homes, also the Titanic Disaster.

Possessed, as he is, of wonderful docility, children of tender years can approach him without the slightest fear of resentment.

THE 'TITANIC' DISASTER FUND

Following the disaster, there was an immediate call to organise a relief fund for the families of passengers and crew, who had been lost with the 'Titanic'.

The London Lord Mayor's Fund was established and with the efforts of fund raising around the country, the fund exceeded £413,200.

Among postcards which exist illustrating fund raising activities, this delightful card shows 'Joe', who collected money for charity, including the 'Titanic' disaster fund, by receiving donations placed in the box strapped to his back.

(M. Bown collection)

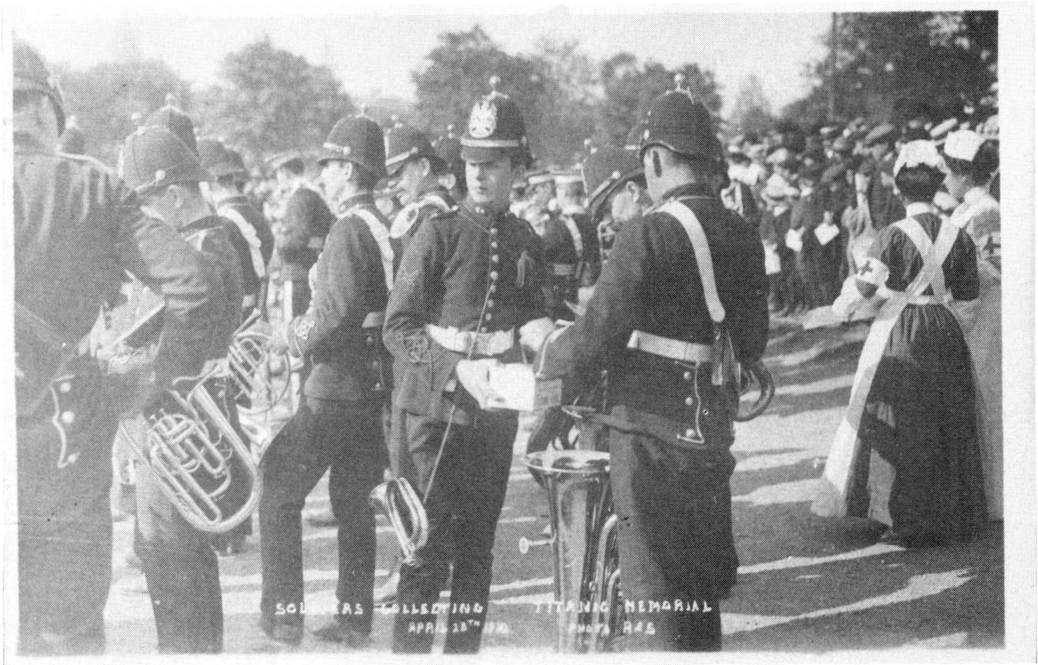

THE 'TITANIC' DISASTER FUND; SOUTHAMPTON

The city of Southampton suffered terribly following the news of disaster, with many families being afflicted by the loss of their loved ones, especially the members of the crew, who had drowned.
The city, set up its own disaster fund and this postcard, postally used 6th May, 1912 and taken from a series, illustrates soldiers collecting for the fund. The date of 28th April suggests that this was photographed at the open-air service held at the Marlands, Southampton to celebrate the return of surviving members of the crew. It was attended by over 50,000 people.

(Published by R. and S., Southampton – R. Simmons collection)

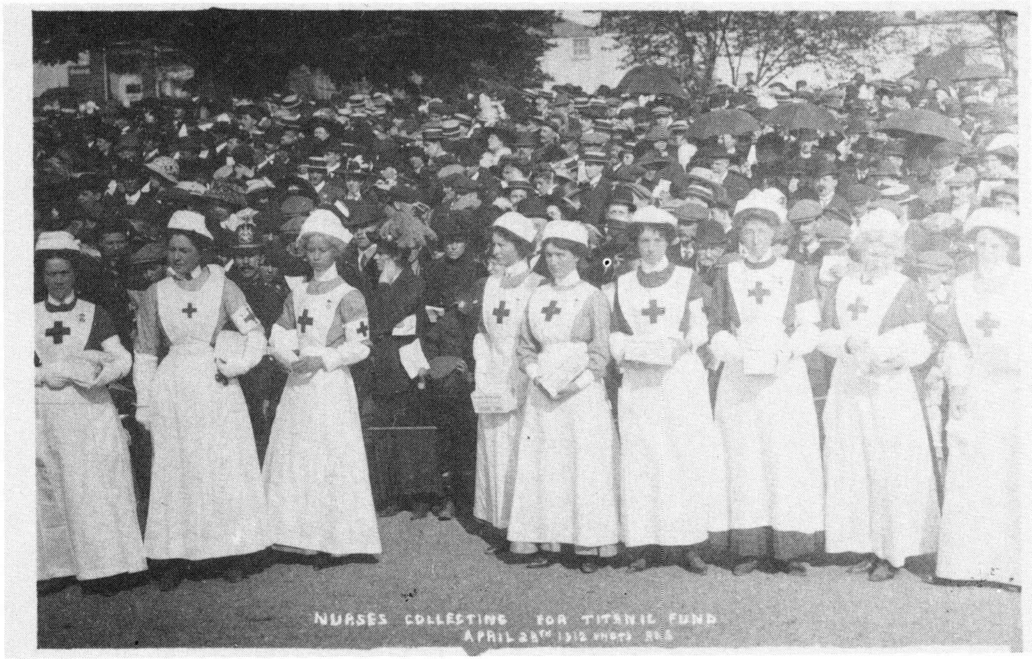

THE 'TITANIC' DISASTER FUND; SOUTHAMPTON

Another postcard in the same series and illustrating nurses collecting for the 'Titanic' fund, set up by the city of Southampton. The proceeds of the fund would have helped to relieve financial hardship for the widows and children of lost crewmen.

Some of the surviving members of the crew arrived in Southampton, after travelling from Plymouth by train, late in the evening of Sunday, 28th April, 1912.

Other members arrived later, to be reunited with their families on Tuesday, 30th April.

(Published by R. and S., Southampton – M. Bown collection)

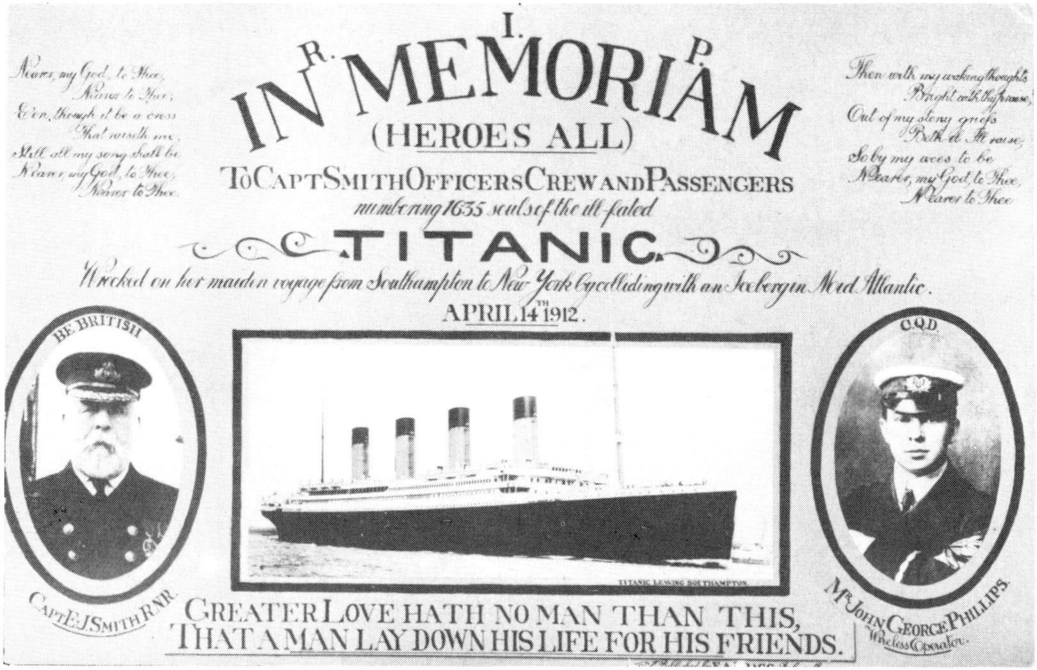

'IN MEMORIAM' POSTCARD

Within three days of the disaster, publishers were producing 'In memoriam' postcards because of the tremendous public interest in the loss of the ship. Numerous varieties were published with some containing factual errors. The postcard illustrated above is one of the best examples of an 'In Memoriam' card and was published by E. A. Bragg of Falmouth.

The photograph of the 'Titanic' was taken when departing from Southampton. John Phillips was the senior radio operator and sent the first C.Q.D. (Come Quickly, Distress) signal at 12.15 a.m. on 15th April, 1912.

(R. Simmons collection)

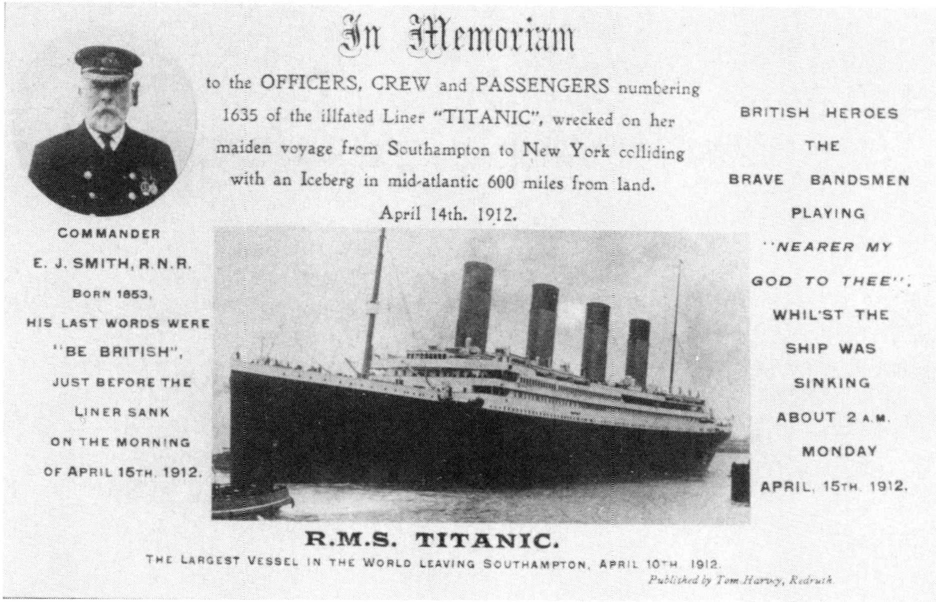

'IN MEMORIAM' POSTCARD

The majority of these cards are edged in black. This card published by Tom Harvey, Redruth, Cornwall gives full details of the disaster and showing the 'Titanic' departing from Southampton.

(M. Bown collection)

In Memory of the **S. S. "TITANIC."** The worlds largest Ship.

Tonnage 46,382
Length 882 ft.
Breadth 92 ft.

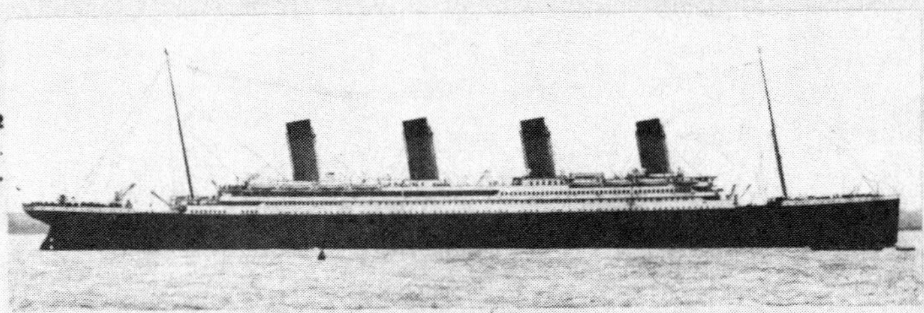

"BE BRITISH."
Capt. Smith's last charge to his men.

WHITE STAR LINER which left

SOUTHAMPTON, APRIL 10TH, 1912.

on maiden voyage to

NEW YORK.

Struck an Iceberg Sunday Night at 11.35 and foundered at 2.20 a.m. Monday, with the loss of 1,635, 705 only being saved.

She went down the Band playing the Hymn "Nearer my God to Thee." Heroes all.

"NEARER MY GOD TO THEE."

Nearer, my God, to Thee,
Nearer to Thee;
E'en though it be a cross
That raiseth me,
Still all my song shall be,
Nearer, my God, to Thee,
Nearer to Thee!

DEBENHAM COWES

'IN MEMORIAM' POSTCARD
Published by Debenham, Cowes, Isle of Wight.
The photograph of the 'Titanic' was taken as the ship proceeded down Southampton Water.
(M. Bown collection)

'IN MEMORIAM' POSTCARD

An unusual multi-view photographic postcard issued after the disaster. The top photograph shows a British warship passing an Atlantic iceberg; the lower photograph shows the 'Titanic' in the Solent on 10th April and the small inset photograph is of the famous British journalist and editor of the Pall Mall Gazette, William Thomas Stead, who was drowned during the disaster. W. T. Stead was on his way to address a peace conference at Carnegie Hall, New York that was to be held on 21st April, 1912.

(Publisher unknown – R. Simmons collection)

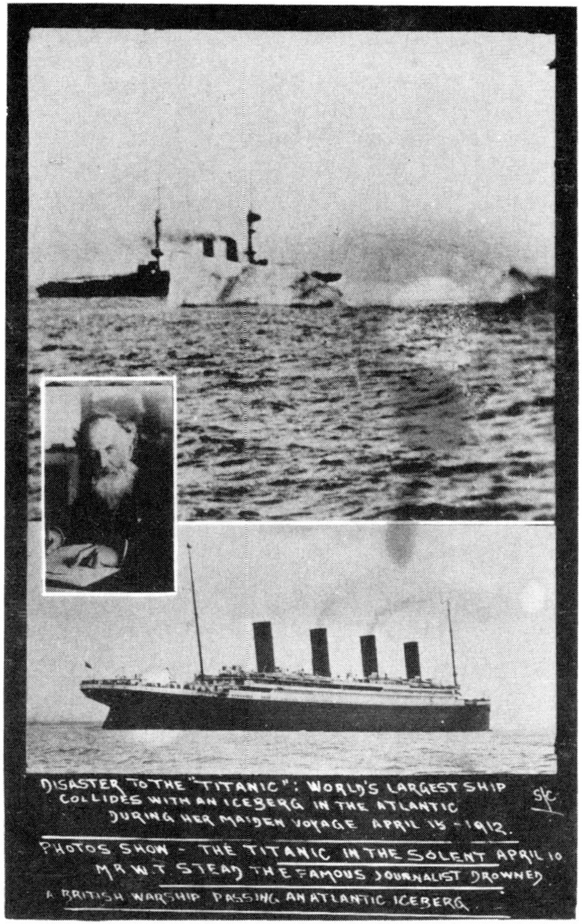

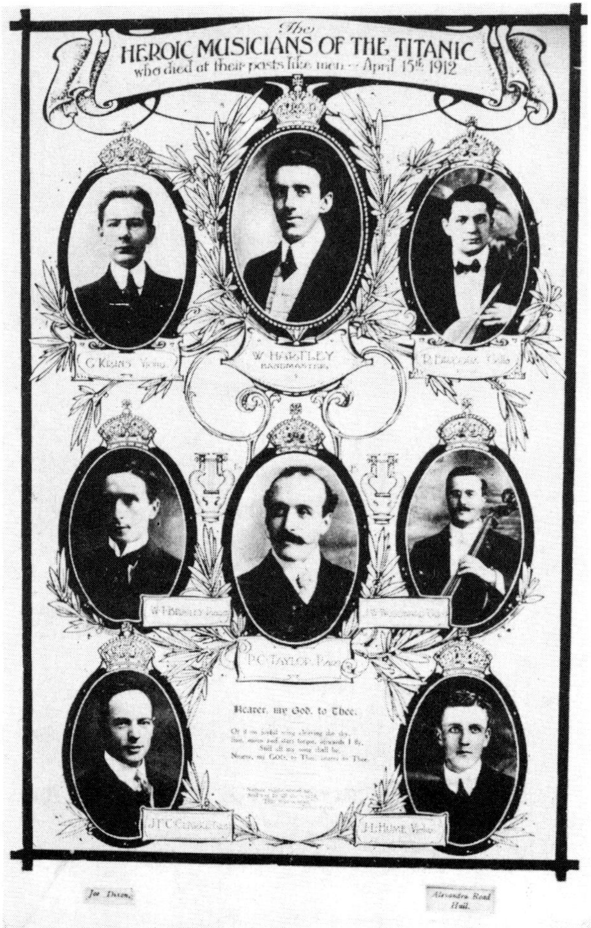

THE HEROIC MUSICIANS OF THE 'TITANIC'

A rare postcard illustrating the members of the ship's orchestra, who all tragically died during the disaster.
Top left to right:
George Krins, violin;
Wallace Hartley, bandmaster;
R. Bricoux, cello.
Middle left to right:
W. Theodore Brailey, piano;
Percy C. Taylor, piano;
J. W. Woodward, cello.
Bottom left to right:
J. F. C. Clarke, bass;
J. L. Hume, violin.

(Published by Joe Dixon, Hull – M. Bown collection)

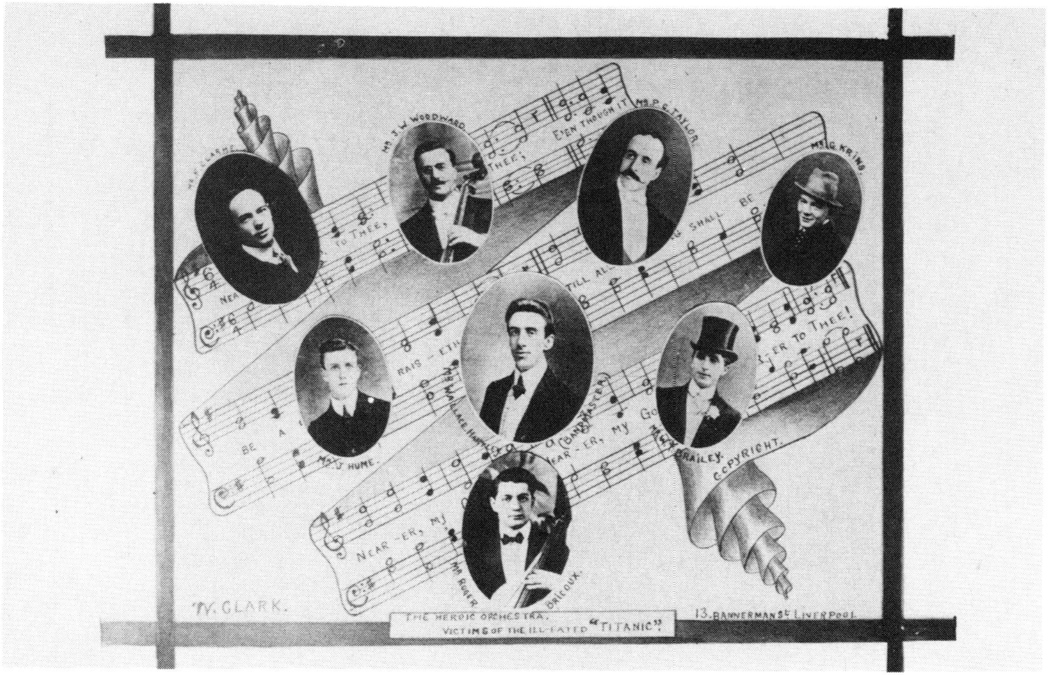

'TITANIC'S' ORCHESTRA

One of the great deeds of heroism that captured the public's imagination was achieved by the members of the 'Titanic's' orchestra led by their bandmaster, Wallace Hartley.
The orchestra continued to play popular tunes, including ragtime right to the very end.
The hymn "Nearer, my God, to Thee!" has been a legend ever since the disaster, as it was believed to have been the last piece of music played by the orchestra before the 'Titanic' took its final dive.
Some survivors also reported that they heard the recessional hymn tune 'Autumn' played during the last moments of the ship.

(Published by W. Clark, Liverpool – R. Simmons collection)

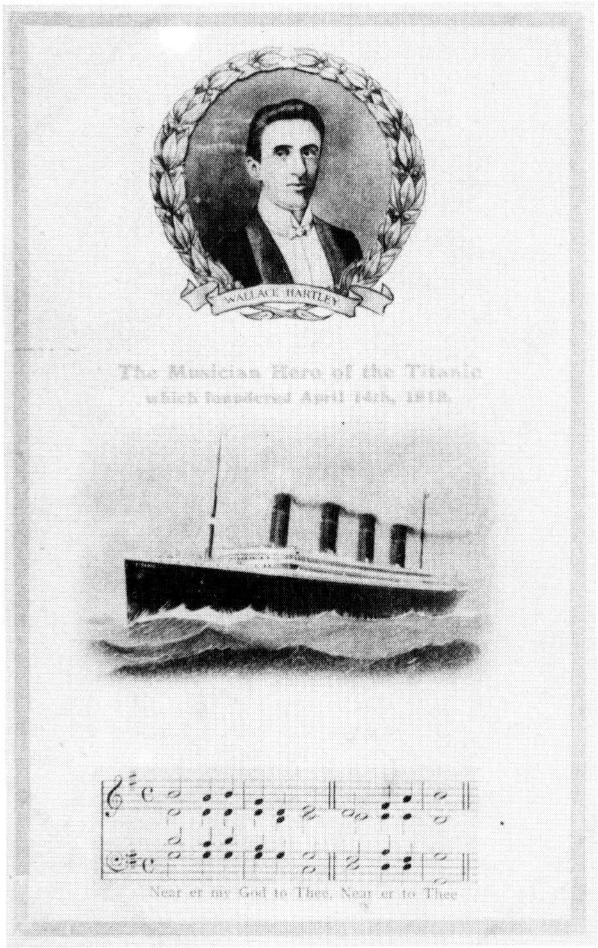

WALLACE HARTLEY,
BANDMASTER OF THE 'TITANIC'

An 'In memoriam' postcard commemorating the heroism of Wallace Hartley (1879 – 1912), bandmaster of the 'Titanic'.
(See also page 93).

(Publisher unknown – M. Bown collection)

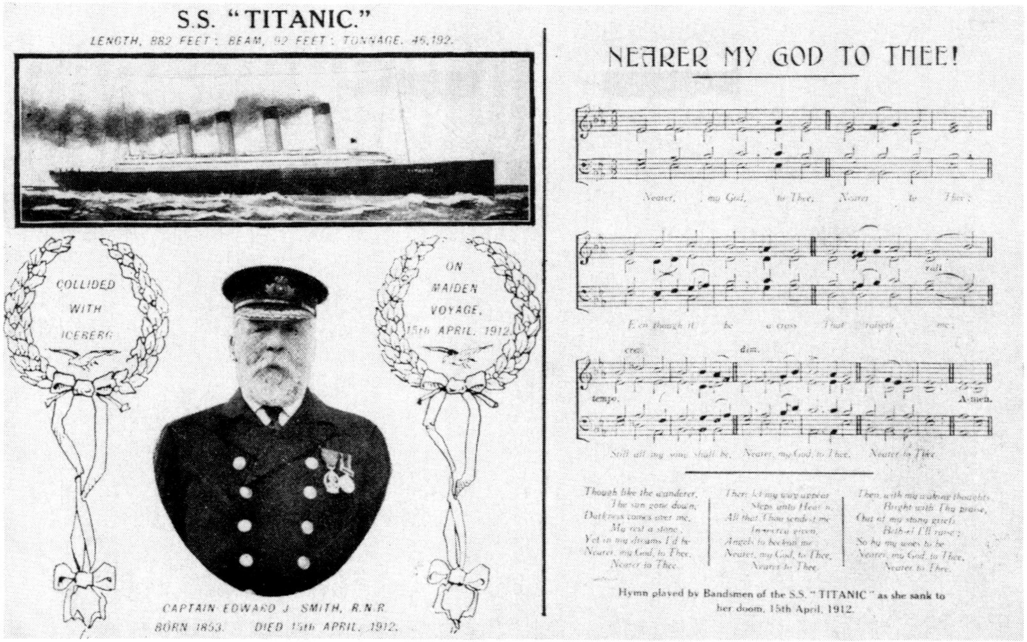

"NEARER, MY GOD, TO THEE!"

A well designed 'In Memoriam' postcard published by Millar and Lang in their "National" series. The inset picture of the 'Titanic' has been reduced from the same picture illustrated on page 75. Additional details are given about the hymn, the collision and Captain Smith.

(R. Simmons collection)

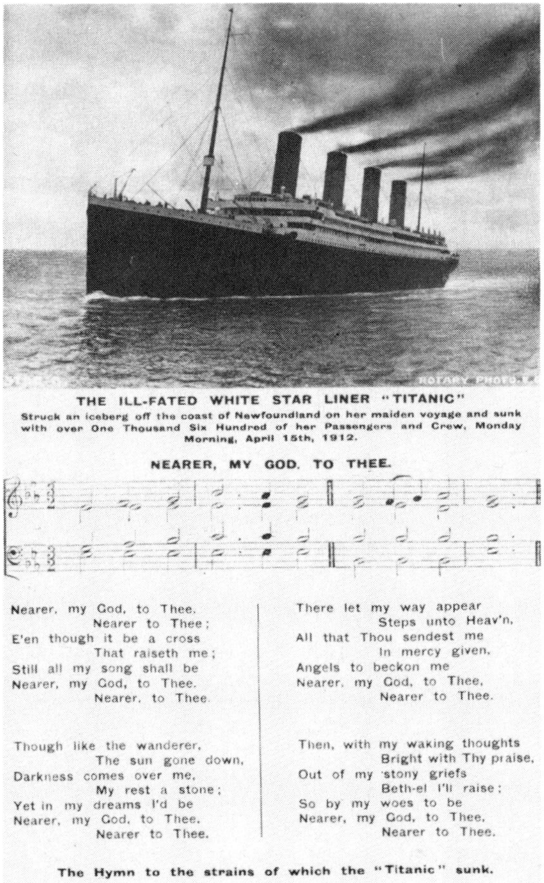

"NEARER, MY GOD, TO THEE!"

Published by Rotary Photographic Company and illustrating the famous hymn. The postcard uses the same photograph of the 'Titanic' departing Southampton on 10th April, 1912. (See page 39). The ship has been superimposed on to a different sea and the artist has drawn a new horizon and added wisps of smoke from all four funnels!

(R. Simmons collection)

"NEARER, MY GOD, TO THEE!"

An exact facsimile of the immortal hymn which appeared on the front page of the 'Daily Mirror' on Saturday, 20th April, 1912, with the headline, "Bandsmen heroes on the sinking 'Titanic' play 'Nearer, My God, To Thee!' as the liner goes down to her doom."

(Publisher unknown – R. Simmons collection)

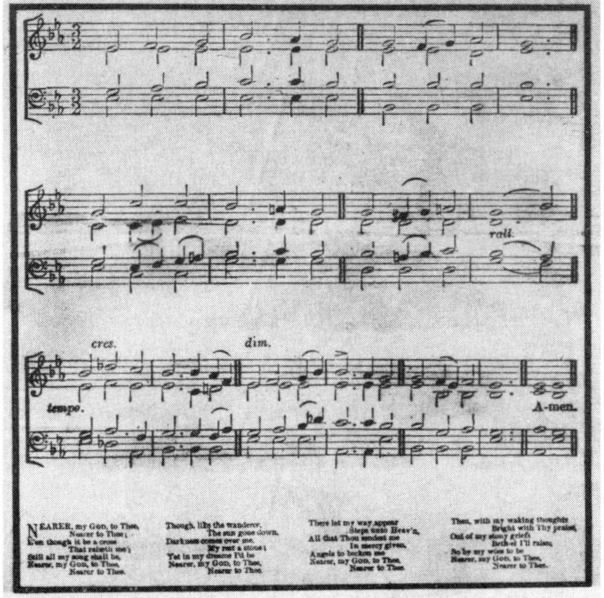

The Daily Mirror

THE MORNING JOURNAL WITH THE SECOND LARGEST NET SALE.

No. 2,649. SATURDAY, APRIL 20, 1912 One Halfpenny.

BANDSMEN HEROES ON THE SINKING TITANIC PLAY "NEARER, MY GOD, TO THEE!" AS THE LINER GOES DOWN TO HER DOOM.

NEARER, my GOD, to Thee,
Nearer to Thee;
E'en though it be a cross
That raiseth me;
Still all my song shall be,
Nearer, my GOD, to Thee,
Nearer to Thee.

Though, like the wanderer,
The sun gone down,
Darkness comes over me,
My rest a stone;
Yet in my dreams I'd be
Nearer, my GOD, to Thee,
Nearer to Thee.

There let my way appear
Steps unto Heav'n,
All that Thou sendest me
In mercy given,
Angels to beckon me
Nearer, my GOD, to Thee,
Nearer to Thee.

Then, with my waking thoughts
Bright with Thy praise,
Out of my stony griefs
Beth-el I'll raise;
So by my woes to be
Nearer, my GOD, to Thee,
Nearer to Thee.

An exact facsimile of the immortal hymn which appeared on the front page of the "Daily Mirror" April 20th. 1912.

By kind permission of the Editor.

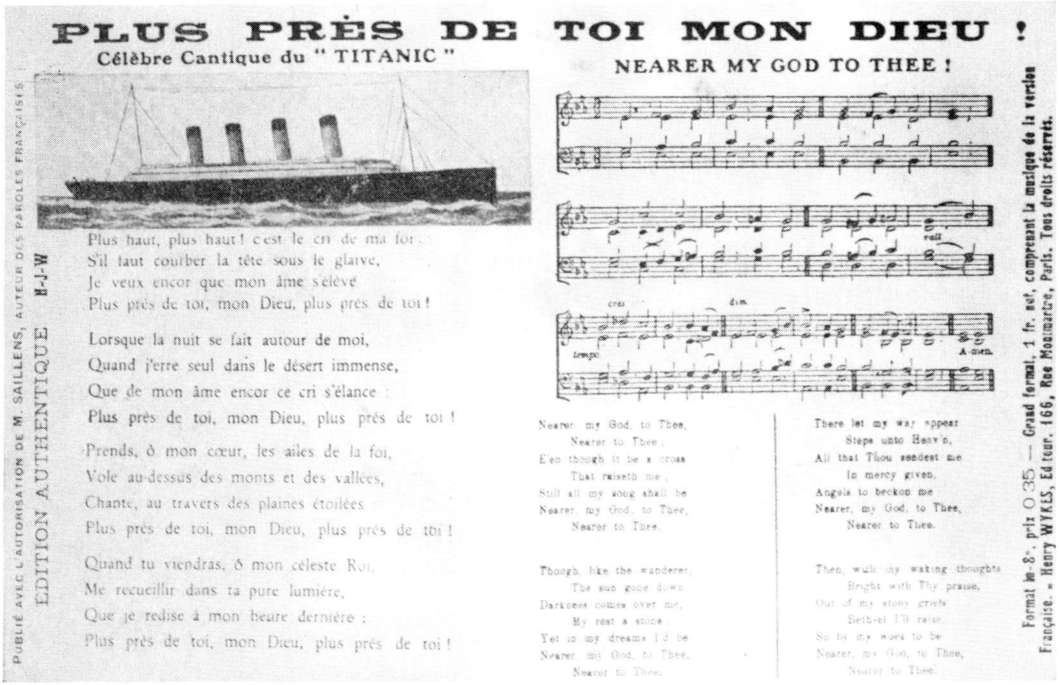

"NEARER, MY GOD, TO THEE!"

An interesting French postcard issued after the disaster with the words of the hymn printed in both French and English.

(Published by Henry Wykes, Paris – M. Bown collection)

BAMFORTH MEMORIAL POSTCARDS (SERIES 21)

Bamforth & Company Ltd., of Holmfirth, near Huddersfield, produced a famous set of six memorial postcards for the 'Titanic' illustrating the 'Titanic' sinking and reproducing verses of the hymn "Nearer, My God, to Thee!", written by Arthur Sullivan. The postcards were published in two varieties: Sepia and black and white.

(R. Simmons collection)

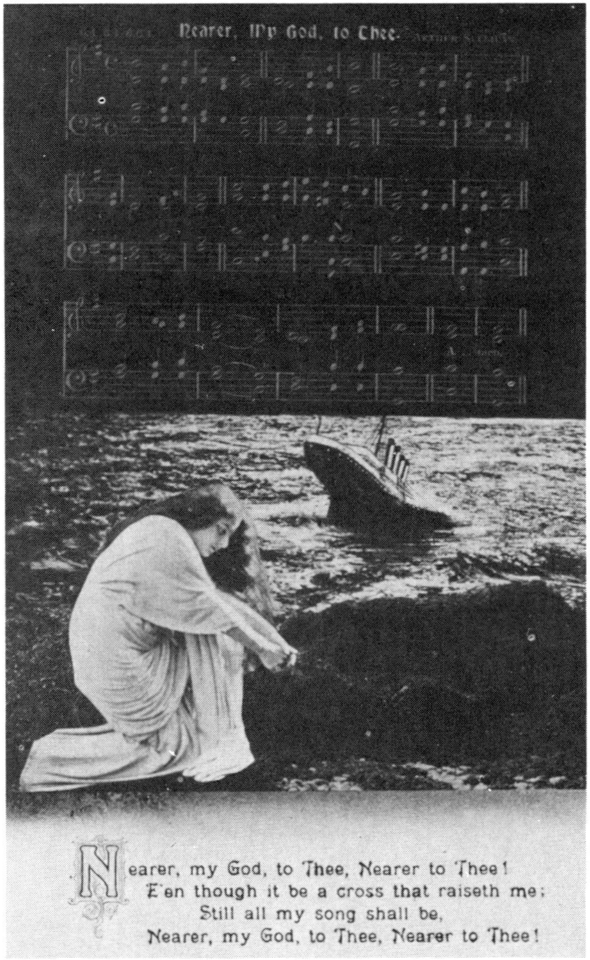

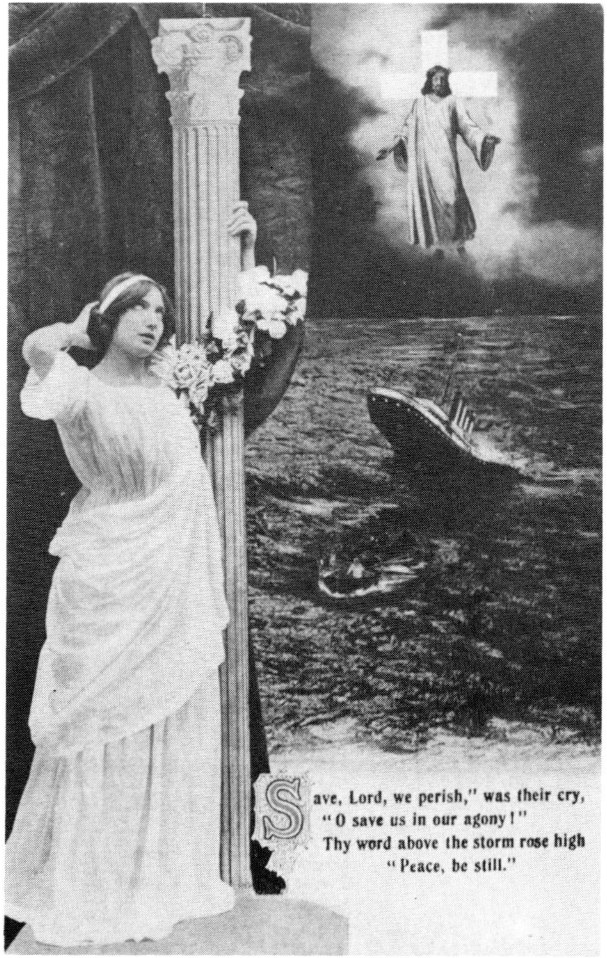

BAMFORTH MEMORIAL POSTCARDS (SERIES 22)

The verse is not from the hymn "Nearer, My God, to Thee!"

(R. Simmons collection)

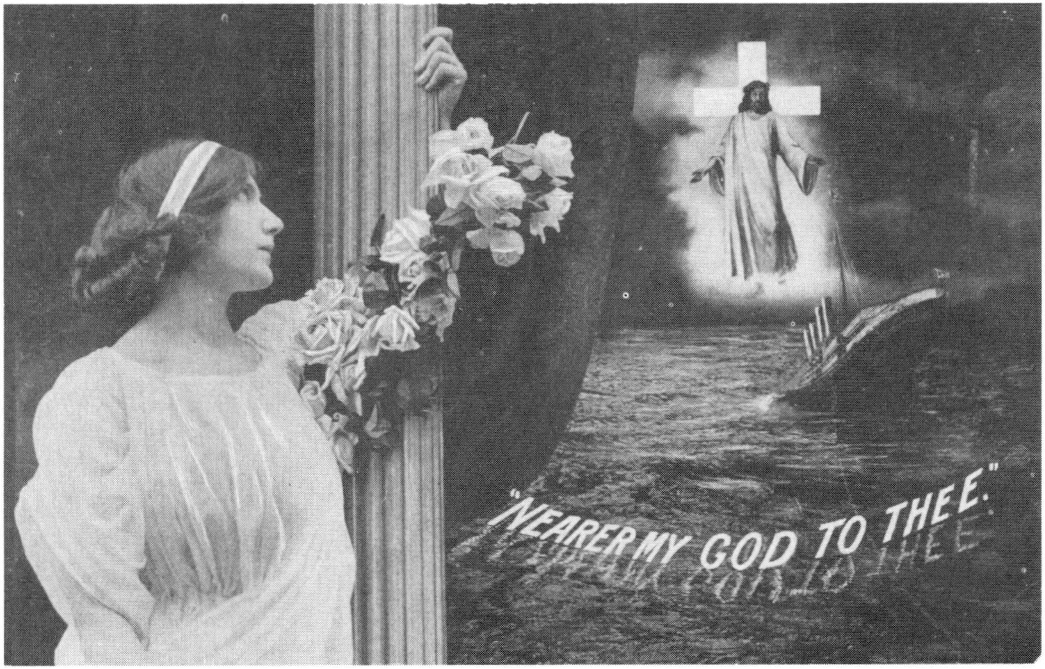

BAMFORTH MEMORIAL POSTCARDS (SERIES 23)

(R. Simmons collection)

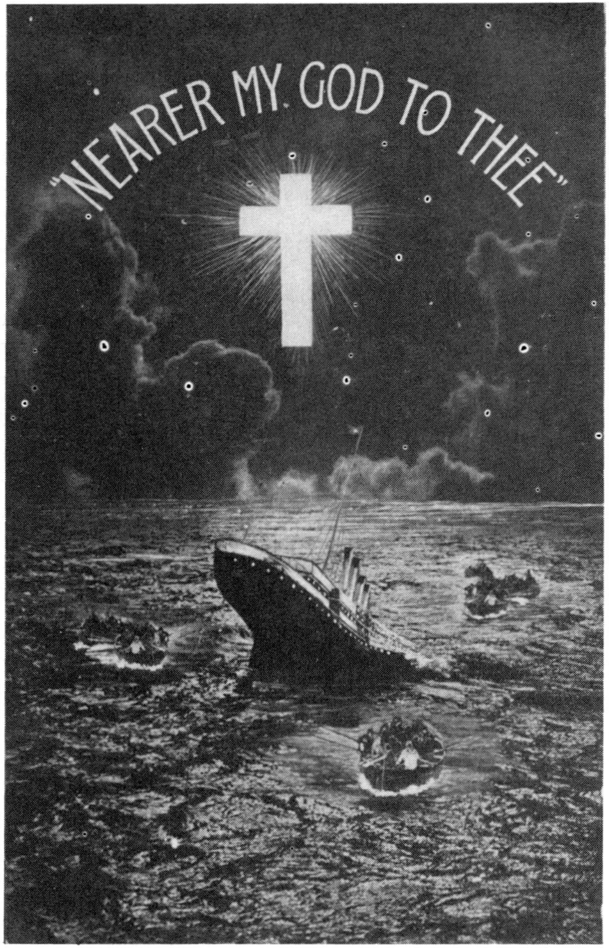

BAMFORTH MEMORIAL POSTCARDS (SERIES 24)

Note the scale of the 'Titanic' compared to the lifeboats surrounding the ship.

(R. Simmons collection)

BAMFORTH MEMORIAL POSTCARDS (SERIES 25)

(R. Simmons collection)

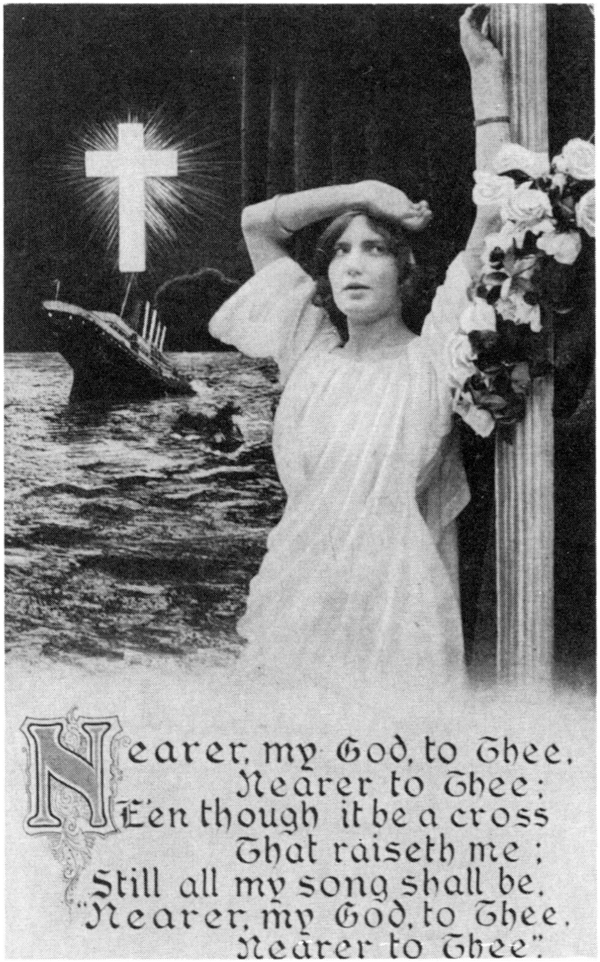

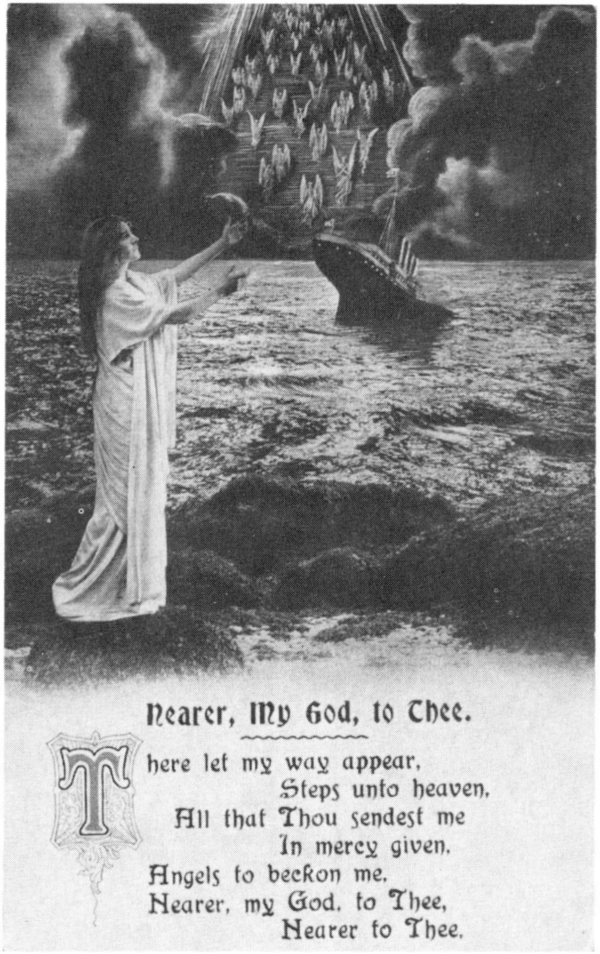

BAMFORTH MEMORIAL POSTCARDS (SERIES 26)
Illustrating verse three of the hymn.
(R. Simmons collection)

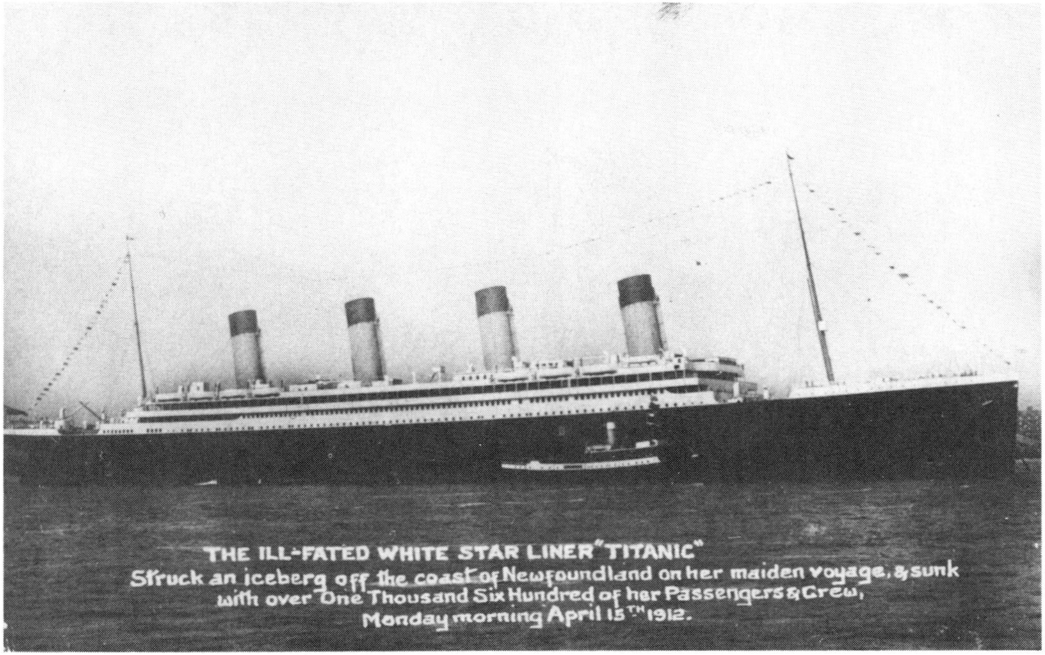

THE 'OLYMPIC' NAMED AS THE 'TITANIC'

Numerous postcards were published following the disaster, and some publishers substituted photographs of the 'Titanic's' sister ship, the 'Olympic'. This could have been the result of publishers having insufficient stocks of 'Titanic' postcards, and not being able to satisfy the demands of the public.

This photograph clearly shows the 'Olympic'. The main difference between the two ships being the open area on the 'Olympic's' forward passenger deck, and the 'Titanic' having an enclosed front forward section on the same deck below the first two funnels.

(M. Bown collection)

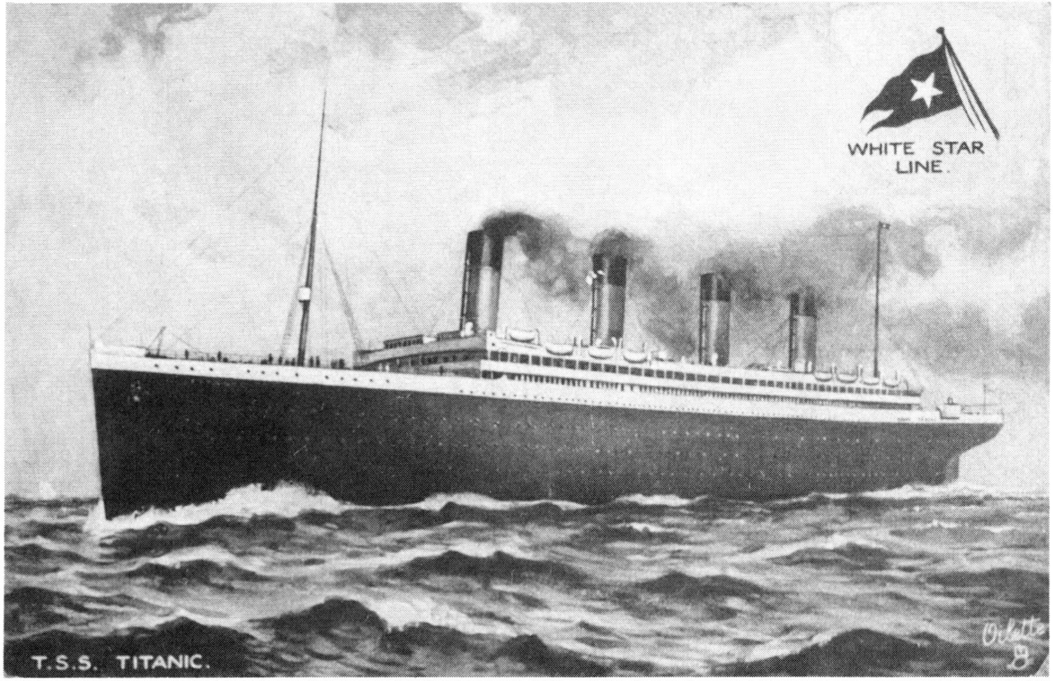

THE 'OLYMPIC' NAMED AS THE 'TITANIC'
A watercolour postcard in Raphael Tuck's Oilette Series;
celebrated Liners – White Star Line, postcard number 9898.
Many different paintings and photographs were published as postcards with many publishers printing details of the disaster on the reverse of the card.
This Tuck postcard also shows the 'Olympic'.

(M. Bown collection)

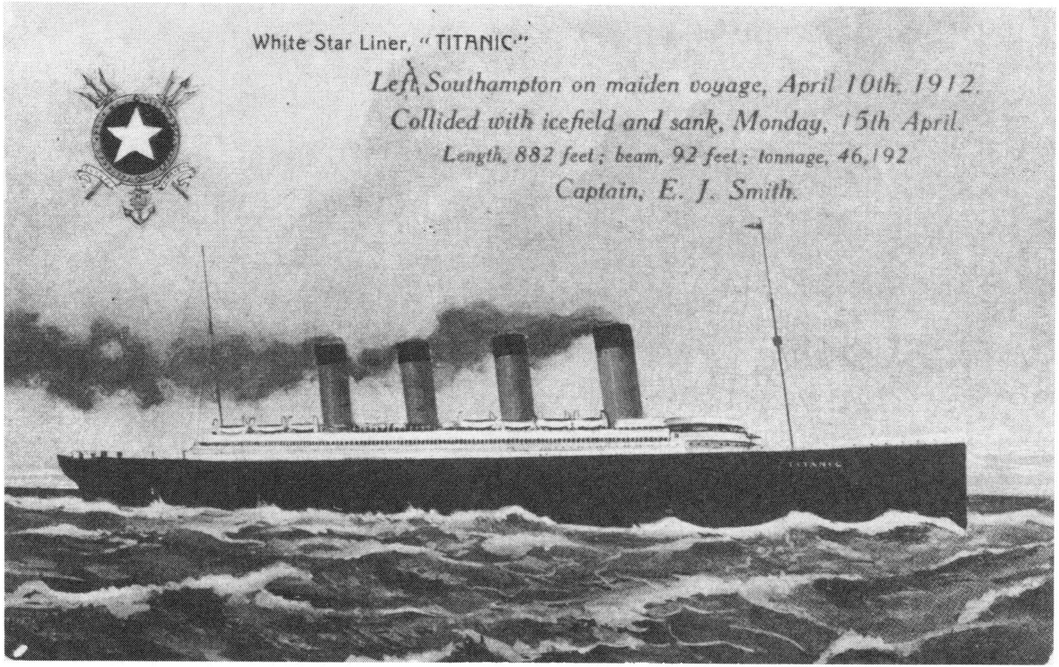

THE 'OLYMPIC' NAMED AS THE 'TITANIC'

This watercolour postcard can be found in two varieties. The rarer postcard has no details of the disaster and the more common card shown above, has the overprinted details above the ship.

The postcard postally used on 19th April, 1912 has the following verse written on message side:–

"Side by side with death He stood, on the trackless ocean wave.
In His arms He gathered them one by one
Jesus, the strong to save and the wild waves sang their requiem,
hushed to eternal rest and this is the message borne to us, He knoweth best.

(Published by Millar and Lang. "National" Series. No. 1756 – R. Simmons collection)

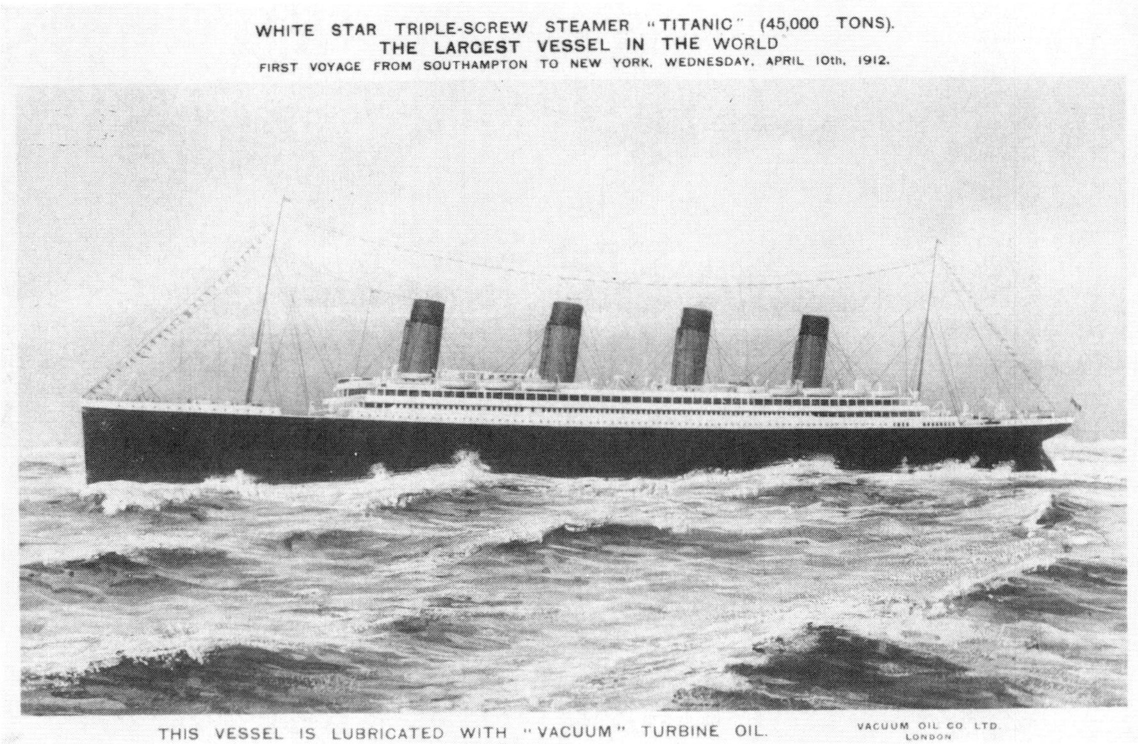

BOOKPOST ADVERTISING CARD

These postcards were originally given away free and now are very collectable.
This advertising postcard issued by The Vacuum Oil Company stating that the 'Titanic' is the largest vessel in the world, is actually illustrated by the 'Olympic'.
An artist has painted in the sea on the photograph, which must have been taken in port, as the ship has been dressed with flags.
Among the other interesting features are the details of the first voyage between Southampton and New York, which are not often seen on postcards.
Tragically, the manager of the 'Vacuum' oil company, Howard Cane who travelled on the 'Titanic' died during the disaster.

(R. Simmons collection)

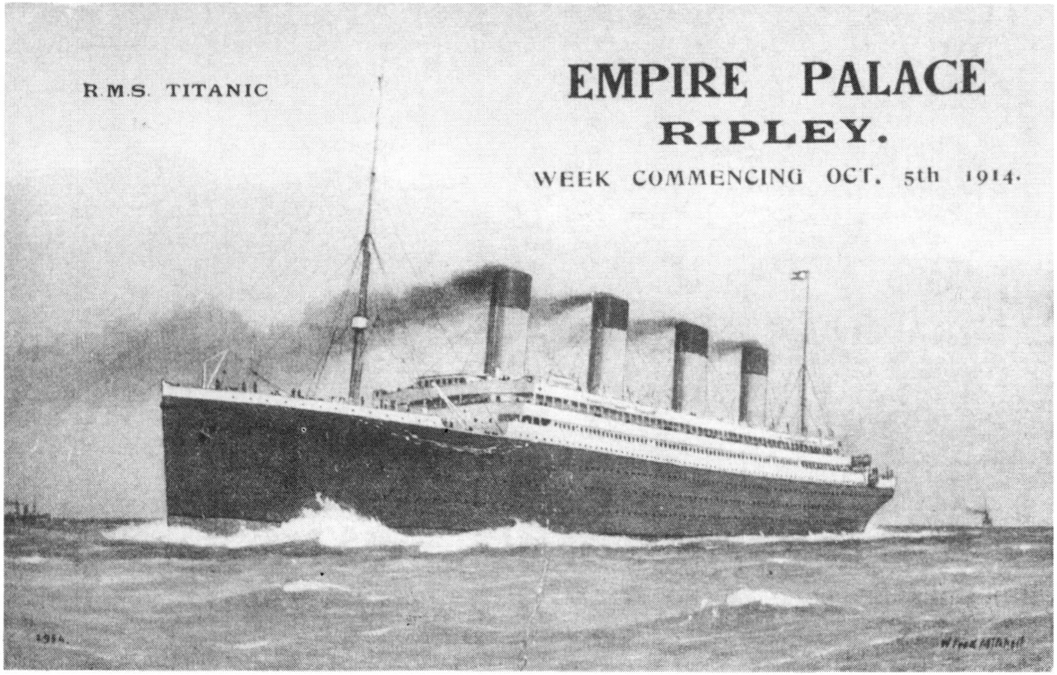

THEATRE ADVERTISING POSTCARD (1)

An advertising postcard based on a watercolour painting of the 'Olympic', announcing the showing of Charles W. and John R. Poole's gigantic reproduction illustrative show, "The Loss of the 'Titanic' ", at the Empire Palace, Ripley, Derbyshire for the week commencing 5th October, 1914.

The same card is known to exist overprinted with different theatres in other parts of the country.

(Published by J. Salmon, Sevenoaks – M. Bown collection)

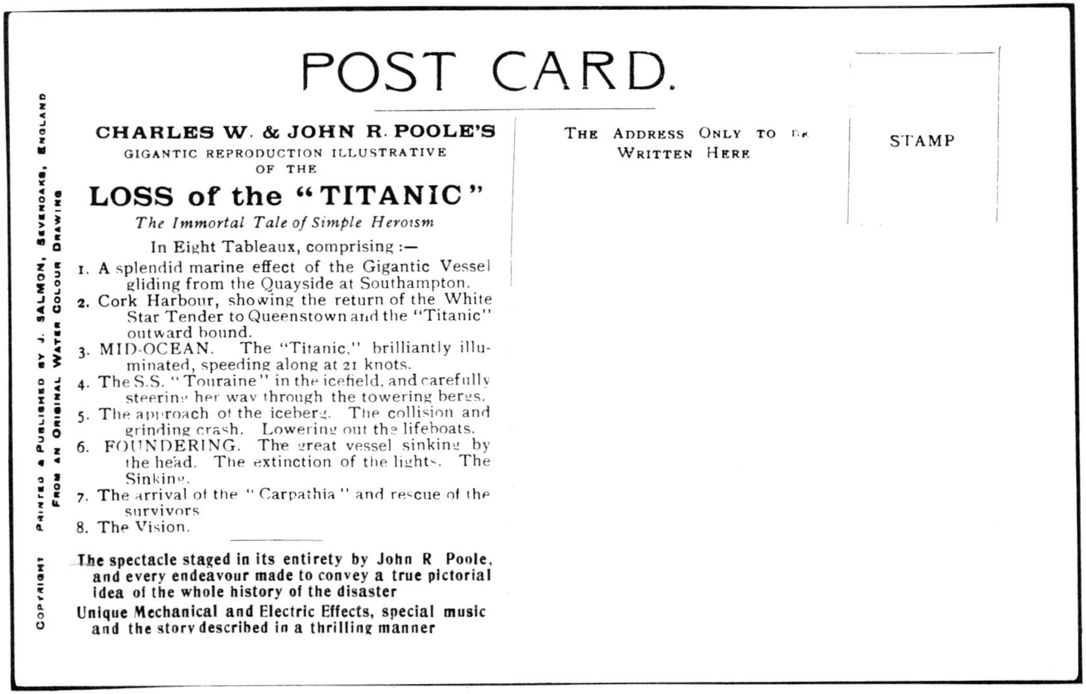

POST CARD.

COPYRIGHT PRINTED & PUBLISHED BY J. SALMON, SEVENOAKS, ENGLAND
FROM AN ORIGINAL WATER COLOUR DRAWING

CHARLES W. & JOHN R. POOLE'S
GIGANTIC REPRODUCTION ILLUSTRATIVE OF THE

LOSS of the "TITANIC"

The Immortal Tale of Simple Heroism

In Eight Tableaux, comprising:—

1. A splendid marine effect of the Gigantic Vessel gliding from the Quayside at Southampton.
2. Cork Harbour, showing the return of the White Star Tender to Queenstown and the "Titanic" outward bound.
3. MID-OCEAN. The "Titanic," brilliantly illuminated, speeding along at 21 knots.
4. The S.S. "Touraine" in the icefield, and carefully steering her way through the towering bergs.
5. The approach of the iceberg. The collision and grinding crash. Lowering out the lifeboats.
6. FOUNDERING. The great vessel sinking by the head. The extinction of the lights. The Sinking.
7. The arrival of the "Carpathia" and rescue of the survivors.
8. The Vision.

The spectacle staged in its entirety by John R Poole, and every endeavour made to convey a true pictorial idea of the whole history of the disaster

Unique Mechanical and Electric Effects, special music and the story described in a thrilling manner

THE ADDRESS ONLY TO BE WRITTEN HERE

STAMP

THEATRE ADVERTISING POSTCARD (2)

The reverse side to the postcard giving details of C. W. & J. R. Poole's unique and thrilling show, utilising mechanical and electrical effects and special music.

(M. Bown collection)

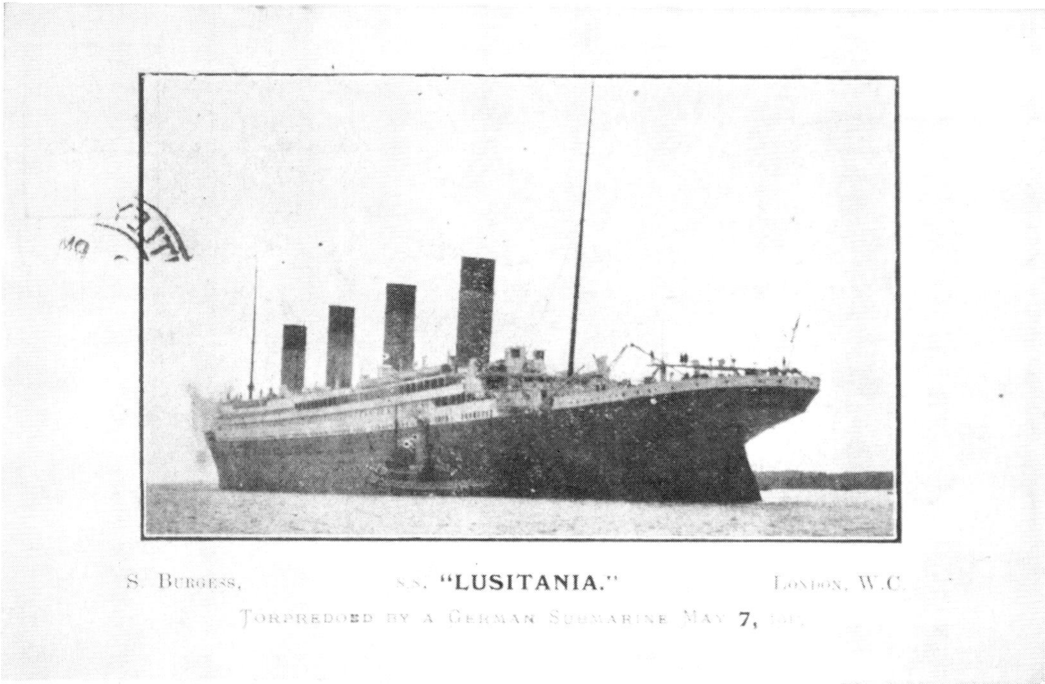

THE 'TITANIC' NAMED AS THE 'LUSITANIA'

This 'In Memoriam' postcard was published to commemorate the loss of the 'Lusitania', torpedoed by a German submarine off the south coast of Ireland on 7th May, 1915.
Amazingly, the ship illustrated is the 'Titanic', photographed when it was departing from Southampton Water on 10th April, 1912.
The enclosed forward section on the passenger deck gives evidence to this fact, and the tug 'Vulcan' is just visible by the ship's side.

(Published by S. Burgess, London – M. Bown collection)

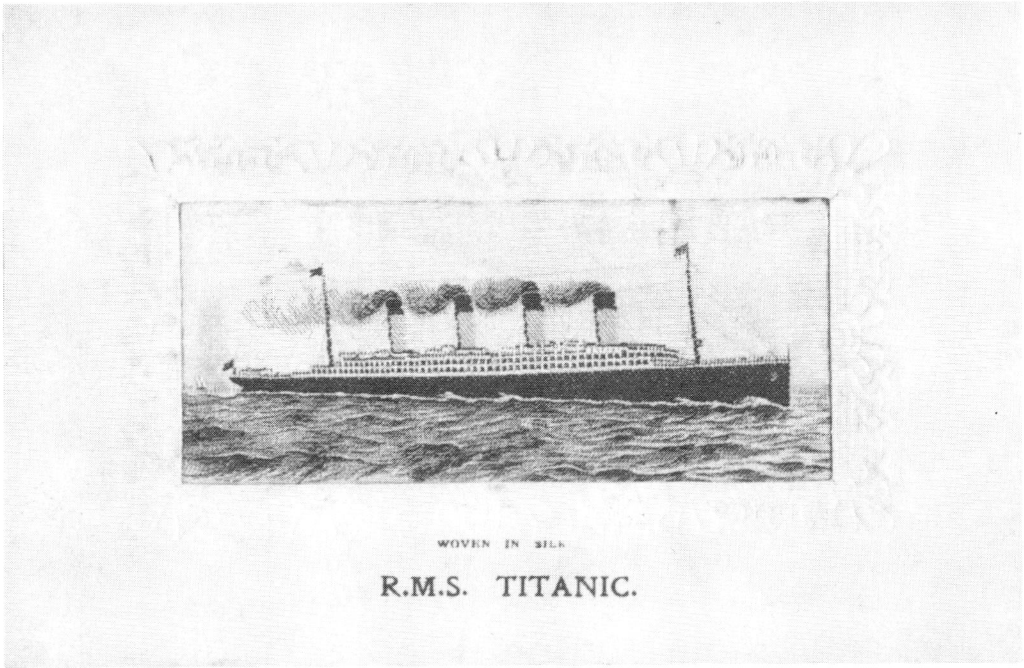

WOVEN SILK POSTCARD

A very collectable woven silk coloured postcard produced by the firm of Thomas Stevens of Coventry.
Similar postcards were also produced by W. H. Grant, also of Coventry.
Woven silks were machine made and had a smooth uniform finish.
Only limited numbers of these postcards were produced and this has contributed to their rarity and value today.

(M. Bown collection)

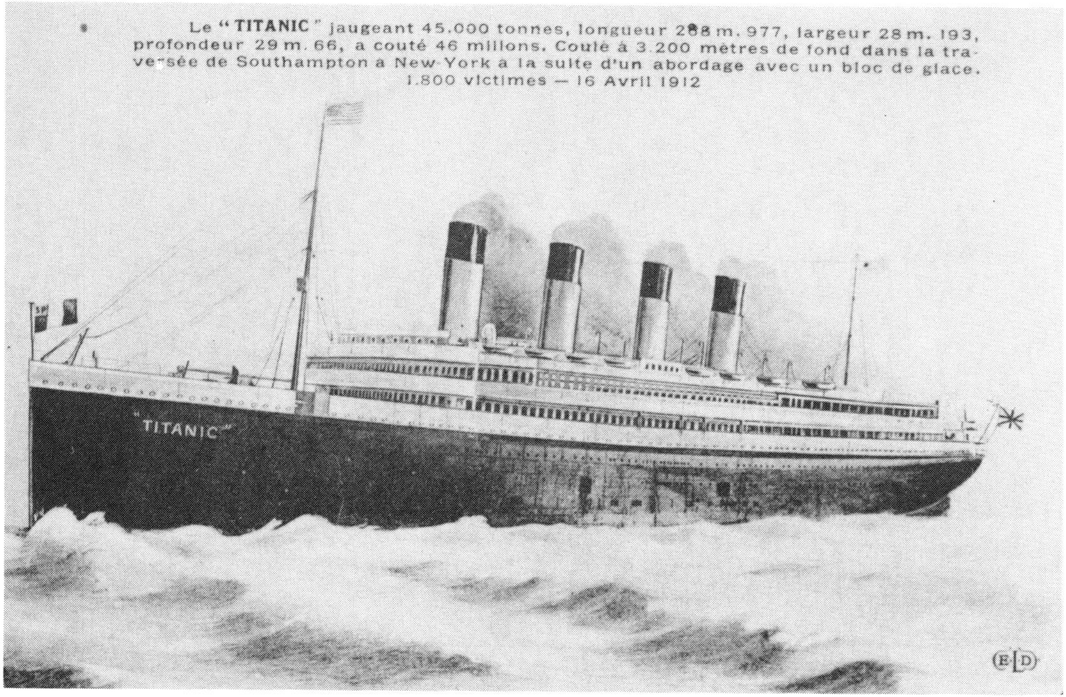

FRENCH 'TITANIC' POSTCARD

An example of a very amateurish French postcard, poorly drawn and giving incorrect details of the disaster. The early reports of the disaster were sketchy and some postcards that were published shortly after the disaster printed the wrong information.

On this postcard, the details list 1,800 victims and the date of the disaster as 16th April, 1912.

(Published by E. L. D., France – M. Bown collection)

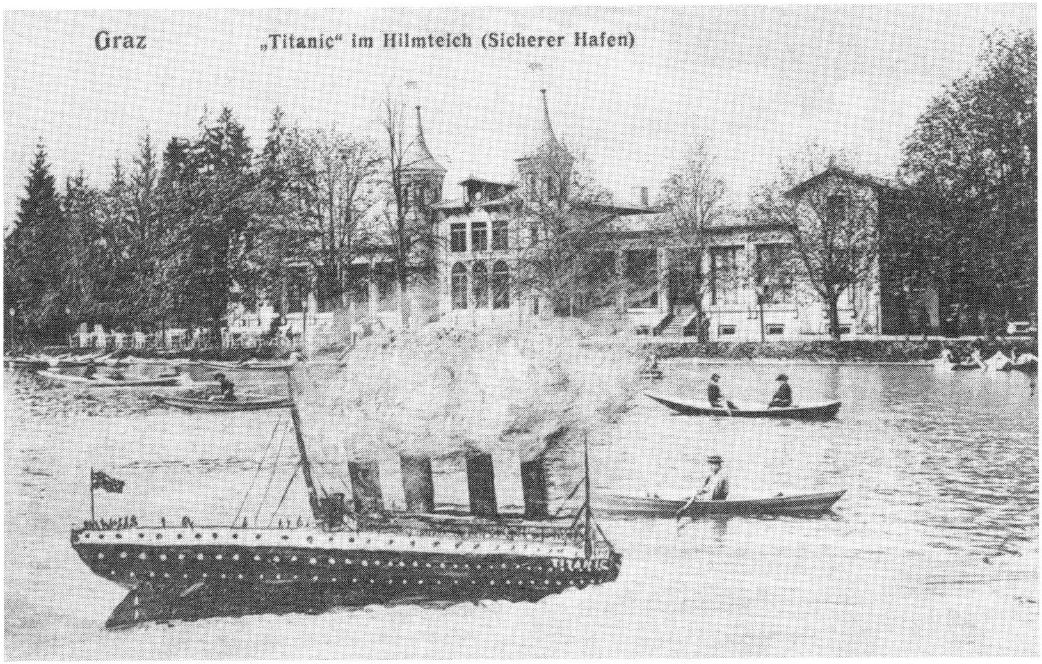

AUSTRIAN 'TITANIC' POSTCARD

A crudely drawn sinking 'Titanic' superimposed on a photograph of the boating lake in Graz, Austria. This very rare and cynical Austrian postcard, postally used on 12th June, 1912, was possibly a political cartoon commenting on the qualities of British Shipbuilding.

(Published by A. Schiauck, Graz. – M. Bown collection)

THE WRECK OF THE 'TITANIC'

by W. Dodd

Proudly, in perfect ease
Waiting to plough the seas,
Rides the 'Titanic'-
Fitted in the highest grade,
A palace superb she made,
The largest of ships for trade,
On the Atlantic.

"Ready" - the word rings out,
Slowly she turns about
While hearts are burning;
Partings now are drawing nigh,
Smiles are masks to be laid by,
But hopes ease the sob and sigh,
Hopes of returning.

Two thousand souls and more
Speed for a distant shore
With thoughts elated;
Ocean calmness makes them glad,
Morn with glorious hues are clad,
Music charms both lass and lad,
Minds are well mated.

By the bulkheads' device
Will she resist the ice?
Quite unthinkable;
Yet passengers while away
the hours; neither grave nor gay
Has a doubt that brings dismay,
"She's unsinkable".

Cold is the starlit night,
No other ship in sight!
In the icefield flow.
Yet swiftly we cross the main,
A new boat must records gain,
But knots and care-nots are vain
In a life's last throe.

"Port helm" - 'twas said too late,
Her keel on the ice doth grate,
The berg looms oe'r us;
Then slowly the knowledge grew
That for passengers and crew
The boats were frail and few!
Death is before us!

Can she be heading down?
Waves may submerge a town,
But is that her end?
Oh husband, mother and child
Trust not to a hope so wild,
Whatever the monster's styled,
On the boats depend.

Women and children first
Into the boats are thrust,
True to tradition;
British Sailors, men of might
Bravely the elements fight,
Heroes save and sink from sight,
Awful condition!

Oh! the terrific blast,
The boilers burst at last!
On the doomed vessel;
Men in masses float around,
Not a boat for them is found,
Fifteen hundred trapped and drowned,
Vainly they wrestle.

The band plays on, at sea -
"Nearer, my God, to Thee",
Their dying refrain.
Comfort take, O ye that weep
For your loved ones in the deep,
Angels precious trophies keep,
They shall live again.

Sunk on her maiden voyage off Cape Race, April 15, 1912

(Publisher unknown – R. Simmons collection)

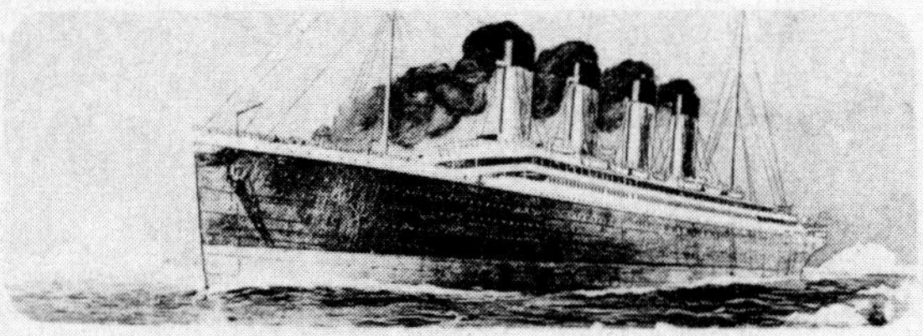

The Wreck of the "Titanic".

Proudly, in perfect ease
Waiting to plough the seas,
Rides the "Titanic".
Fitted in the highest grade,
A palace superb she made,
The largest of ships for trade
On the Atlantic.

"Ready" the word rings out,
Slowly she turns about
While hearts are burning;
Partings now are drawing nigh,
Smiles are masks to be laid by,
But hopes ease the sob and sigh.
Hopes of returning.

Two thousand souls and more
Speed for a distant shore
With thoughts elated;
Ocean calmness makes them glad,
Morn with glorious hues are clad,
Music charms both lass and lad,
Minds are well mated.

By the bulkheads' device
Will she resist the ice?
Quite unthinkable;
Yet passengers while away
The hours, neither grave nor gay
Has a doubt that brings dismay,
"She's unsinkable"

Cold is the starlit night,
No other ship in sight!
In the icefield flow.
Yet swiftly we cross the main,
A new boat must records gain,
But knots and care-nots are vain
In a life's last throe.

"Port helm" - 'twas said too late,
Her keel on the ice doth grate,
The berg looms oer us;
Then slowly the knowledge grew
That for passengers and crew
The boats were frail and few!
Death is before us!

Can she be heading down?
Waves may submerge a town,
But is that her end?
Oh husband, mother and child
Trust not to a hope so wild,
Whatever the monster's styled,
On the boats depend.

Women and children first
Into the boats are thrust,
True to tradition;
British Sailors, men of might
Bravely the elements fight,
Heroes save and sink from sight,
Awful condition!

Oh! the terrific blast,
The boilers burst at last!
On the doomed vessel;
Men in masses float around,
Not a boat for them is found,
Fifteen hundred trapped and drowned.
Vainly they wrestle.

The band plays on, at sea
"Nearer, my God, to Thee",
Their dying refrain.
Comfort take, O ye that weep
For your loved ones in the deep,
Angels precious trophies keep,
They shall live again.

W. Dodd

Sunk on her maiden voyage off Cape Race, April 15, 1912

THE WRECK OF THE 'TITANIC'

by A. Stott

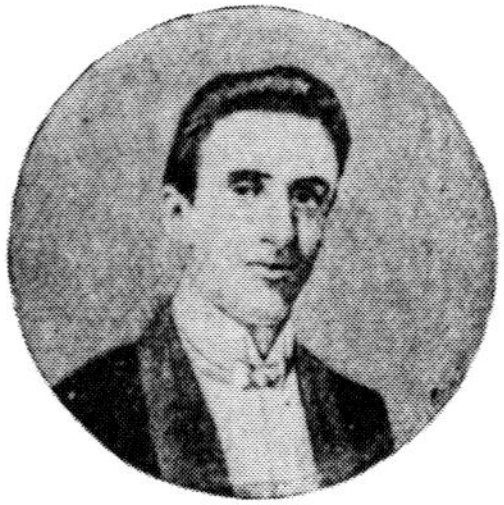

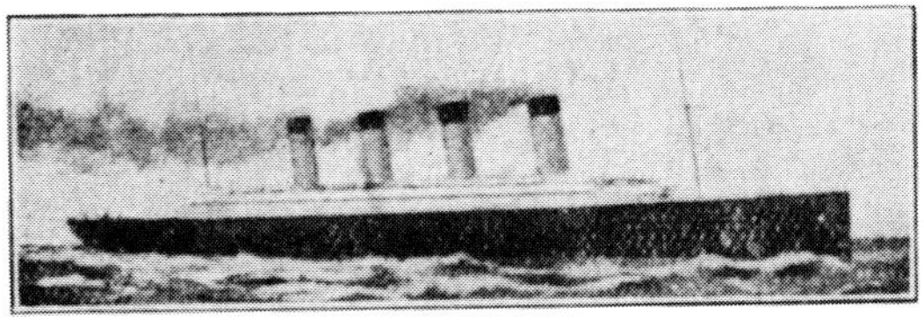

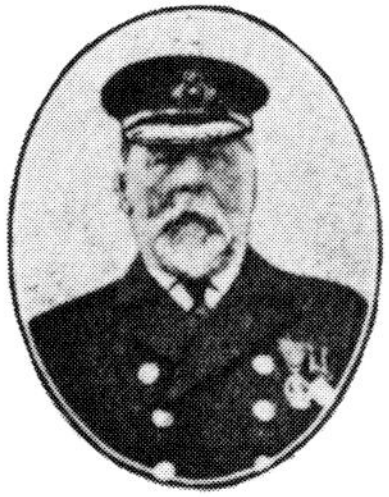

"As they slumber in the sea, may they find sweet rest in Thee."

On a morning bright in April,
The Titanic sailed away,
In her stately pride and glory,
With all hearts so blithe and gay.

The captain he had said "good-bye,"
Unto his wife and child,
To steer his ship across the foam,
O'er the Atlantic wild.

That night the captain's daughter fair,
Prayed in her silent home,
That God would guide and keep him safe,
While on the raging foam.

And as the ship sped on her way,
There was no thought of fear;
But O, how little did they think,
That death was then so near.

She was a floating paradise,
As lovely as could be.
Her beauty and her splendour,
Were the envy of the sea.

It e'en was said she could not sink,
This monarch of the deep;
But O, how vain now her brave hearts,
Down in the ocean sleep.

She ploughed the waves magnificently,
Until one Sunday night,
From the "crow's nest" came the warning,
That something was in sight.

"Port your helm" the officer cried,
Alas! it was too late,
For the ship had struck an ice-burg.
And soon would meet her fate.

The captain standing on the bridge,
Gave orders for the boats,
Whilst the band was playing softly,
In sweet melodious notes.

His voice rang clear throughout the ship,
"Women and children first,"
And all who dare to disobey,
To die and suffer must.

The sea was calm the night was clear,
The stars above shone bright,
And to see the great ship sinking,
Was a said and awful sight.

Then here's to the gallant members
Of that famous little band,
Who, though the ship was sinking,
Made such a noble stand.

Away on the lonely ocean,
Out on the cold dark sea,
They played for ever sweetly,
"Nearer, my God, to Thee."

And here's to young Jack Phillips,
Though only but a boy,
For his message o'er the waters,
To many a heart brought joy.

Away on the lonely billows,
There on the cold bleak wave,
He stuck to his post of duty,
Just like an hero brave.

And still he kept on sending
For help, in the wire-less room,
And just as the vessel foundered,
The brave lad met his doom.

To-night a mother mourns the loss,
Of her fair boy so brave,
For her bonny lad lies sleeping.
Out in a sailor's grave.

And here's honour to the captain,
So kind, so true, and bold,
Who stuck to his post of duty,
Amid the ice and cold.

Still there he stood upon the bridge,
A thoughtful prayer was given,
That all who went down with the ship,
Would meet again in heaven.

The last act of the captain
Was to save a baby boy;
As he gave it to the mother,
It filled her heart with joy.

And then for Murdock he did ask,
He was the ships first mate,
And a voice then answered softly
That he had met his fate.

Away he swam back to his ship,
As she was going down,
And he too went down with her,
In glory and renown.

We mourn the loss of our hero,
May he rest in peaceful sleep,
With the ship he loved so dearly,
Down in the ocean deep.

Away in a lonely mansion,
Dwells a widow and child so fair,
With broken hearts now sighing,
For the captain is missing there.

Oh God! in our great sorrow,
Do Thou our comfort be,
Keep watch and guide our sailors,
From the perils of the sea.

There are many hearts now mourning,
For the ones that they loved best,
As they think of an ocean graveyard,
Of the loved ones now at rest.

With sorrow and with sadness,
We think of the ship at sea,
May the souls that went down with her,
Ever find sweet rest in Thee.

This poem was originally published as a Book Postcard and priced one penny.
(R. Simmons collection)

LOSS OF THE TITANIC.

In sorrowful Memory of her gallant Crew, drowned in mid-ocean, April 15th, 1912.

OH! why all this sad consternation
That spreads over Southampton fair,
And sends such a thrill through the nation
Filling so many hearts with despair?
The wondrous Ship the Titanic
With her life-giving heroes so true
Ne'er thought death awaited so closely,
Though danger was near, they well knew.

CHORUS.

In the cold arms of death they sleep,
Their loss many friends will mourn;
Many relations are weeping
For those now dead and gone;
Their voices are now quite still,
They are free from all sorrow and pain,
No more will their loved ones see them,
Or welcome them home once again.

The crash in mid-ocean was awful,
The ship into an iceberg ran;
"At once save the women and children,"
Was the order for every man.
The brave ship's noble Captain,
To save every life vainly tried;
But many fulfilling their duty,
Sank with the vessel and died.

We grieve for the homes so afflicted,
For the loved ones so suddenly lost,
For the husbands, the brothers, and children,
Who died standing at duty's post.
We feel for the dear wives and children,
We ask for them God's tender care,
And trust Him to help and support them,
And help them their sorrow to bear.

" THE LOSS OF THE 'TITANIC' "
One of the many songs composed in memory of the 'Titanic', and printed on a postcard.
(Publisher unknown – M. Bown collection)

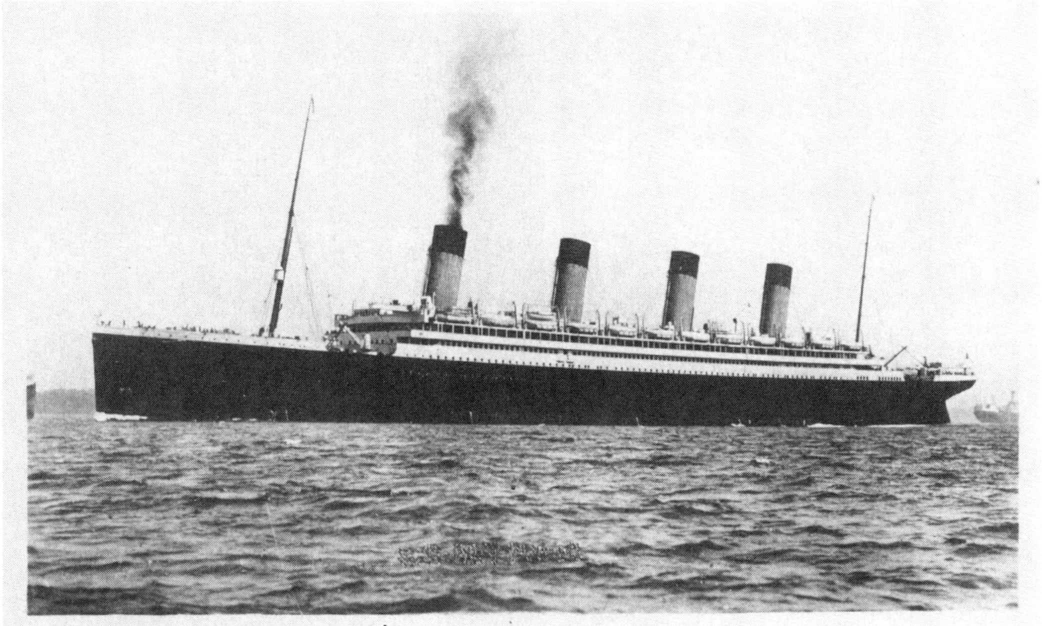

1002 C. R. Hoffman R.M.S. "OLYMPIC." 46,439 Tons.

THE COURTS OF INQUIRY Two Courts of Inquiry were held to investigate the loss of the 'Titanic'. The American Inquiry chaired by Senator William Smith was held in New York between 19th April to 25th May, 1912 and the British Inquiry chaired by Lord Mersey was held in London between 2nd May and 30th July, 1912. The main conclusions at both Courts of Inquiry were:– The speed of the 'Titanic' had been too fast, taking into account the reported existence of extensive ice in the area. The ship had insufficient lifeboats for passengers and crew, some being difficult to launch and others being launched without their full complement on board. Captain Lord of the 'Californian' was also criticised for not investigating the distress rockets seen by his ship. As a result of the findings of the British Inquiry, the Board of Trade introduced new safety measures, which have become universal. These measures included sufficient lifeboats on every ship for all passengers and crew, regular boat drills and a 24-hour radio watch to be maintained. The illustration shows the 'Olympic' after her major refit undergone in 1912-13, costing £250,000, and showing her additional lifeboats.

(Published by C. R. Hoffman, Southampton – R. Simmons collection)

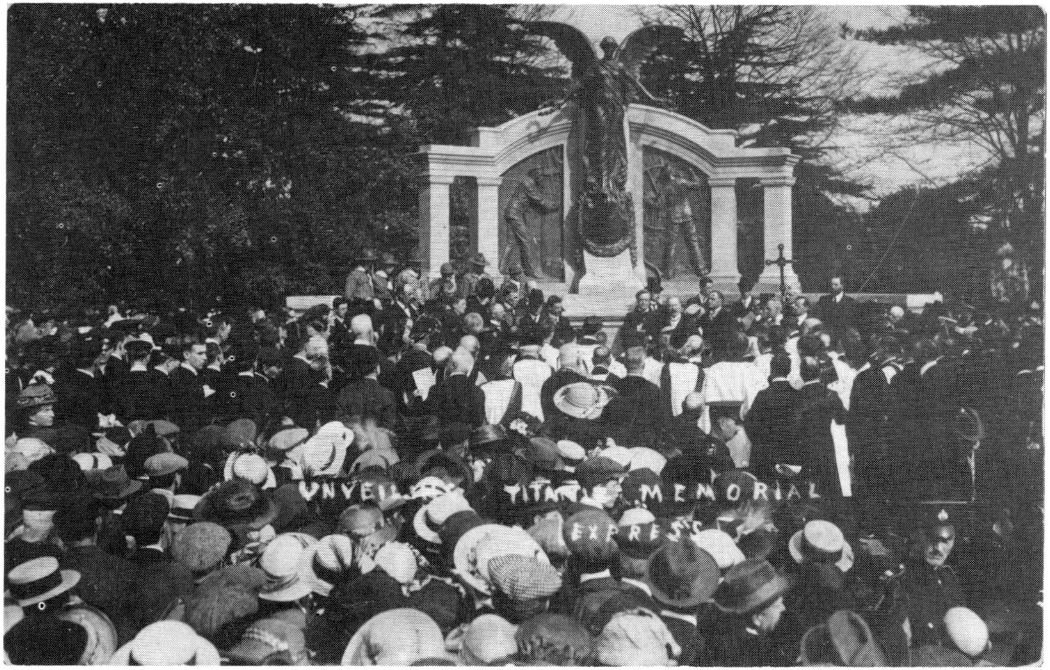

THE UNVEILING OF THE 'TITANIC' ENGINEER'S MEMORIAL, SOUTHAMPTON

The memorial to all the brave engineers, who perished on the 'Titanic', is sited in East Park, Southampton. For the unveiling ceremony, the memorial was covered by a large Union Jack, which was formally unveiled by Sir Archibald Denny on 22nd April, 1914, just over two years later from the date of the disaster. It was estimated that over one hundred thousand people were present for the ceremony.

(Publisher unknown – M. Bown collection)

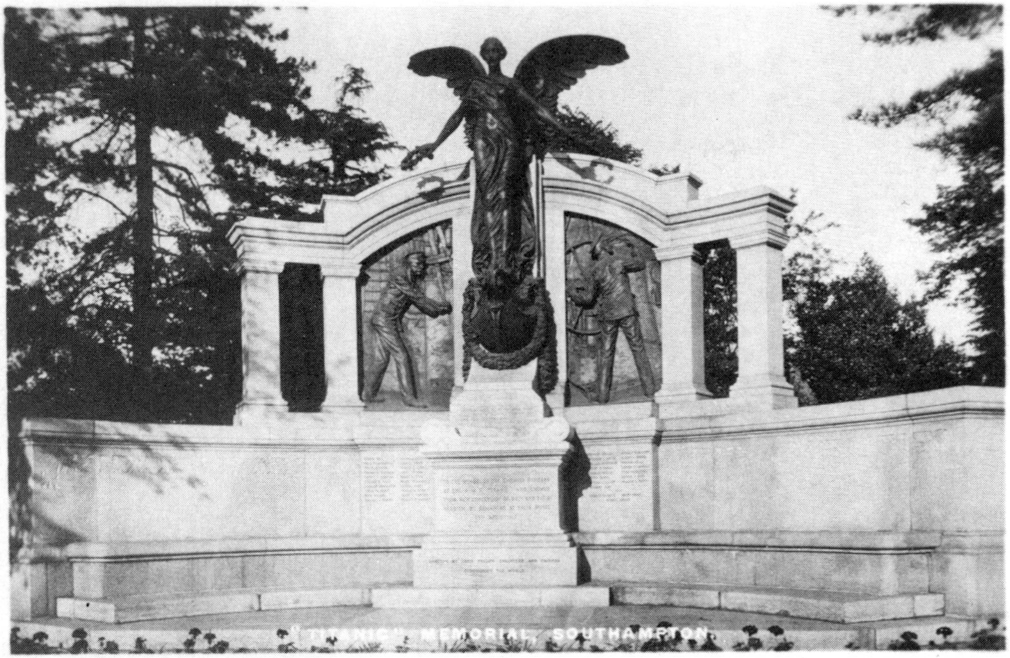

THE 'TITANIC' ENGINEER'S MEMORIAL, SOUTHAMPTON

Published by Pelham in their real photographic series and showing this beautifully sculptured memorial in more detail. Many postcards were produced both locally and nationally illustrating the memorial. After the unveiling ceremony, iron railings were placed in front of the memorial. The railings were removed in 1940 for the war effort and never replaced.

(M. Bown collection)

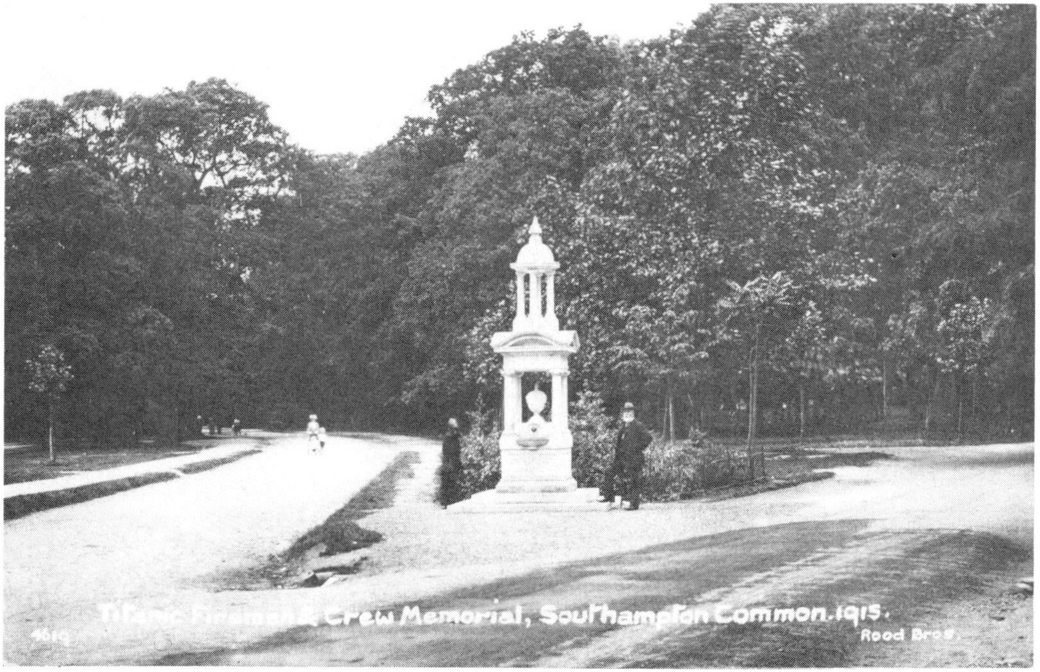

'TITANIC' FIREMEN AND CREW MEMORIAL, THE COMMON, SOUTHAMPTON

This memorial was erected to the memory of the firemen, sailors and stewards of the 'Titanic', and was originally located on The Common in Southampton.

A special fund had been organised by the people of Southampton and the memorial was officially unveiled by Mr. Bullions Moody, Treasurer to the fund, on 27th July, 1915.

(Published by Rood Bros. – M. Bown collection)

'TITANIC' FIREMEN AND CREW MEMORIAL, SOUTHAMPTON

The memorial was sculptured from Portland stone and also served as a drinking fountain.
The centre urn is now missing and following vandalism to the memorial, it was removed for its protection to the ruins of Holy Rood Church in 1972. The church was badly destroyed during the Second World War and has been kept as a memorial to the Merchant Navy. The 'Titanic' memorial was restored and cleaned in 1982.

(Published by G. D. Courtney, Southampton – M. Bown collection)

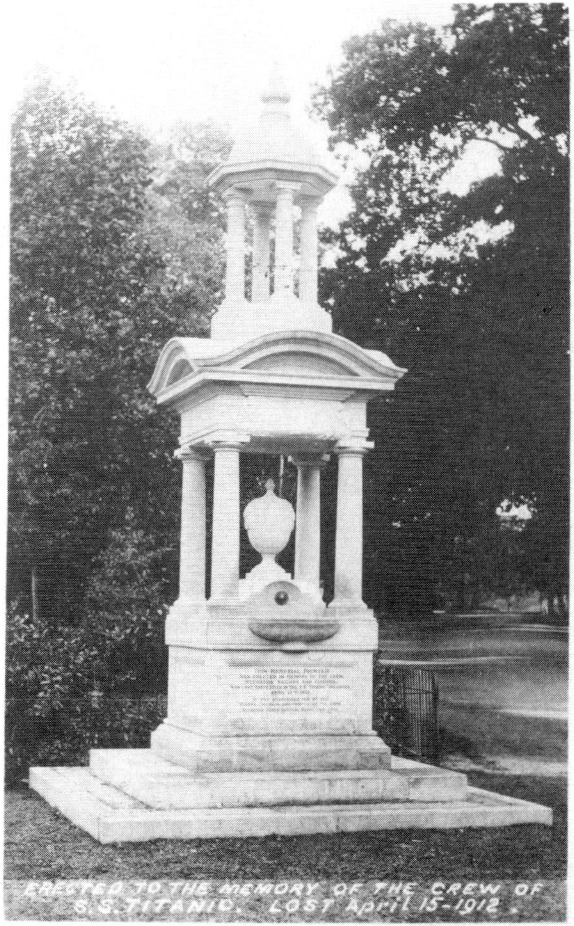

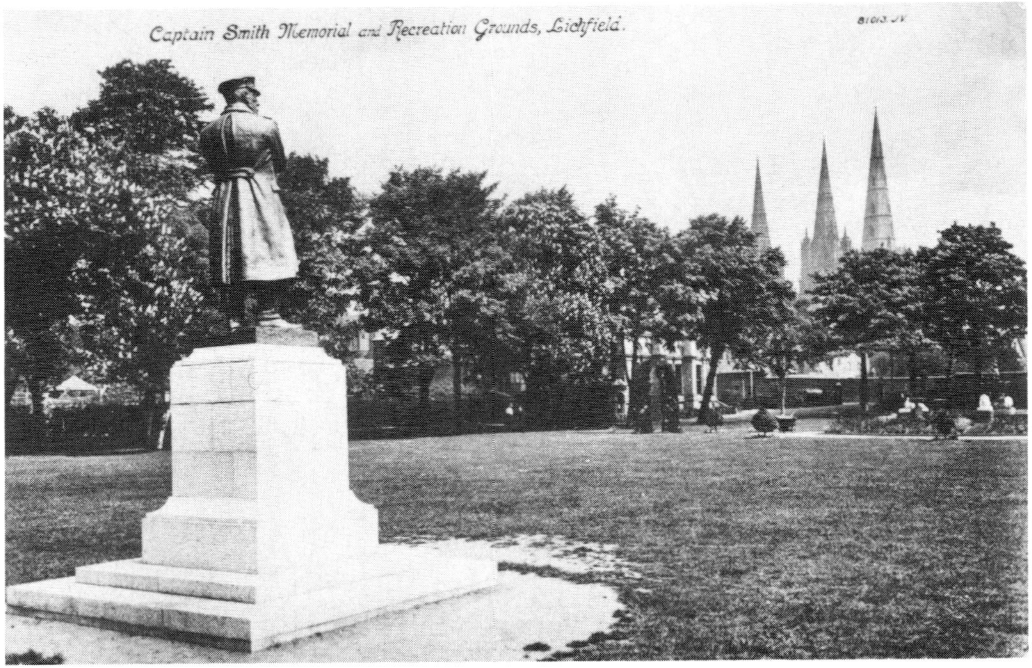

CAPTAIN SMITH'S MEMORIAL, LICHFIELD, STAFFORDSHIRE

The memorial is made of bronze and stands 7′ 8″ on a plinth of Cornish granite.
It was sculptured by Lady Kathleen Scott (1878-1947), widow of Captain R. F. Scott, C.V.O., R.N., the famous Antartic explorer.
The formal unveiling of the statue took place on 29th July, 1914 by Helen Smith, daughter of Captain Smith, and also in the presence of Lady Scott.
On the front of the plinth the memorial plate reads:
Cdr. Edward John Smith, R.D., R.N.R. Born 27th Jan. 1850. Died 15th April 1912.
Bequeathing to his countrymen the memory and example of a great heart, a brave life and a heroic death. "Be British".

(Published by Valentines – M. Bown collection)

THE GRAVE OF WALLACE HARTLEY

The body of the 'Titanic's' bandmaster, Wallace Hartley who was only thirty three years old, was returned to England on 12th May, 1912, on board the White Star liner, 'Arabic'.

He was buried with full honours in his home town of Colne, Lancashire on 18th May, 1912.

A fine monument also exists in the town park in Colne.

(Publisher unknown – M. Bown collection)

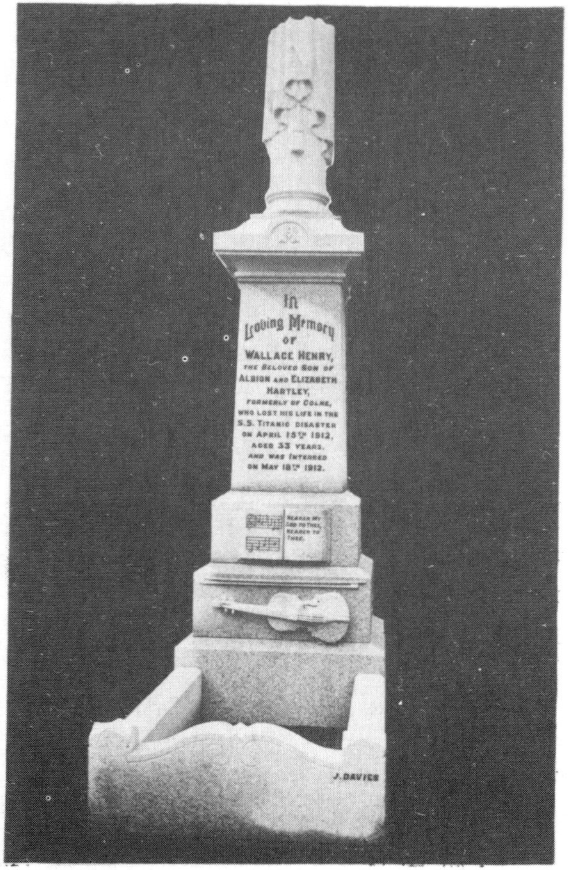

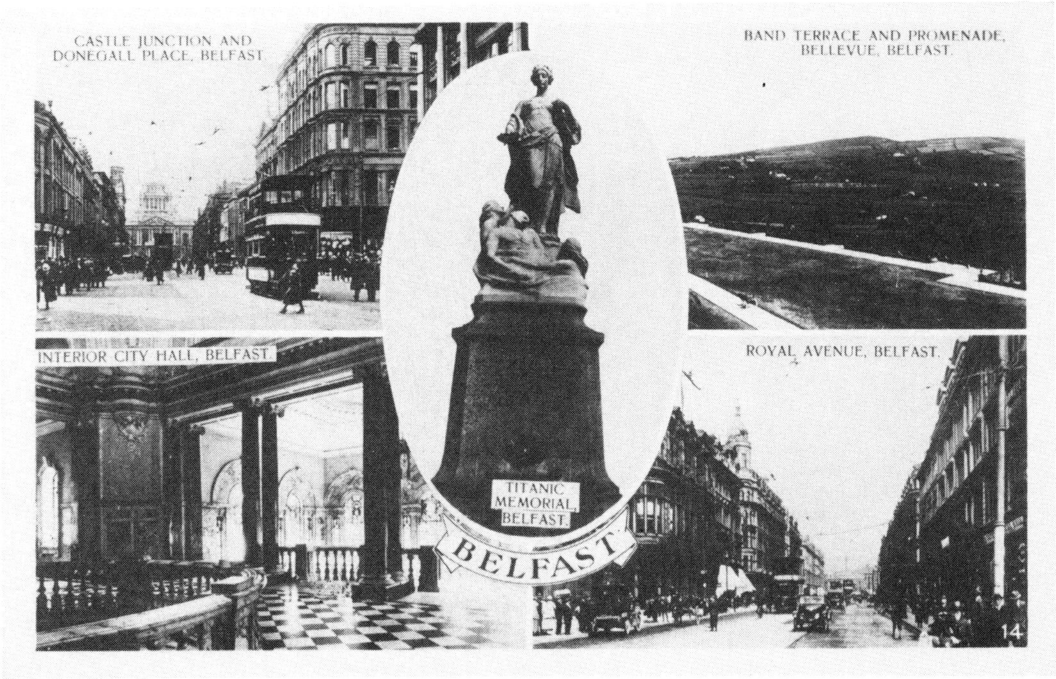

THE 'TITANIC' MEMORIAL, BELFAST

A multi-view postcard illustrating the statue originally sited at the front of Belfast City Hall. The statue was dedicated in 1920 and shows two mermaids aiding a victim of the disaster. The statue has now been resited on the eastern side of the City Hall.

(M. Bown collection)

In Memory of

The stupendous White Star Liner, 45,000 tons,

S. S. "TITANIC,"

Which foundered in the North Atlantic, after Collision with an Iceberg,

ON MONDAY, APRIL 15TH, 1912, AT 2-20 A.M.,

Involving the loss of 1,514 Lives.

CAPTAIN SMITH'S CALL---"BE BRITISH!"

Mourn for the Brave, who met their fate,
As British heroes always do;
Courageous, resolute, and cool,
To training and traditions true.

CHRONOLOGY

Early 1907	The Chairman of White Star Line, J. Bruce Ismay discusses with Lord Pirrie, Chairman of Harland and Wolff, Belfast, a plan to build three luxury liners to provide a weekly service from Southampton to New York.
1st July, 1907	Order placed with Harland and Wolff to build three ships. The 'Olympic' (no. 400) and the 'Titanic' (no. 401) to be built first, followed by the 'Gigantic' (renamed 'Brittanic') later.
1st Jan., 1909	'Olympic's' keel laid.
31st March, 1909	'Titanic's' keel laid.
20th Oct., 1910	'Olympic' launched.
late May, 1911	Completion of 'Olympic'.
29th–30th May, 1911	Sea Trials of 'Olympic'.
31st May, 1911	Launch of 'Titanic'; 'Olympic' departs Belfast.
14th June, 1911	Maiden voyage of 'Olympic' from Southampton.
20th Sept., 1911	Collision between 'Olympic' and H.M.S. 'Hawke'.
6th Oct., 1911	'Olympic' returns to Belfast for repairs.
24th Feb., 1912	'Olympic' returns to Belfast for further repairs to propeller.
2nd April, 1912	Sea Trials of 'Titanic'.
2nd April, 1912	8.00 p.m. 'Titanic' departs Belfast.
4th April, 1912	'Titanic' arrives Southampton.

CHRONOLOGY CONTINUED

10th April, 1912	Noon	Maiden voyage of 'Titanic' from Southampton.
	6.30 p.m.	Arrives at Cherbourg.
	8.10 p.m.	Departs Cherbourg.
11th April, 1912	11.30 a.m.	Arrives at Queenstown.
	1.30 p.m.	Departs Queenstown.
14th April, 1912	11.30 p.m.	Lookout reports iceberg. Avoiding action taken.
	11.40 p.m.	Strikes iceberg on Starboard side.
15th April, 1912	12.15 a.m.	Distress call sent (CQD). Position 41° 46′ N, 50° 14′ W.
	12.25 a.m.	'Carpathia' answers call. Alters course to 'Titanic'.
	12.45 a.m.	'Titanic' sends S.O.S. distress call. First boat lowered (No. 7) with only 20 people.
	1.55 a.m.	Last rigid boat lowered.
	2.05 a.m.	Two collapsible lifeboats lowered.
	2.20 a.m.	'Titanic' finally sinks, with the loss of 1503 lives.
	4.00 a.m.	'Carpathia' arrives at scene of disaster.
	8.30 a.m.	'Carpathia' departs for New York having picked up 703 survivors and 14 lifeboats. 'California' arrives to search for further survivors.
18th April, 1912	9.30 p.m.	'Carpathia' arrives in New York.
17th April – 8th June, 1912		Four ships chartered by White Star recover 328 bodies from the area of the disaster. 209 are taken to Halifax, Nova Scotia and the remainder are buried at sea.
19th April – 25th May, 1912		American Court of Inquiry, New York.
2nd May – 30th July, 1912		British Court of Inquiry, London.

ACKNOWLEDGEMENTS

The authors are indebted to the following, without whom this book would not have been possible:

Bamforth & Co. Ltd., Holmfirth, Huddersfield for their kind permission to reproduce the set of six 'In Memoriam' postcards in their song card series.

The Directors and Staff of Sidgwick and Jackson Ltd. for their help and advice.

Sally Mancell for design and artwork for the cover.

Steve Benz for his original idea, enthusiasm and editorial.

All the postcards illustrated are owned by and selected from the author's collections.